The LAKES & CUMBRIA Cook Book

A celebration of the amazing food & drink on our doorstep.
Featuring over 30 stunning recipes.

The Lakes & Cumbria Cook Book

First edition printed in 2018 in the UK.

ISBN: 978-1-910863-30-5

Thank you to: Simon Rogan - L'Enclume and Kevin Tickle - Forest Side

Compiled by: Anna Tebble, Kelly Markell and Gavin McArthur

Written by: Katie Fisher

Photography by: Tim Green
www.timgreenphotographer.co.uk

Edited by: Phil Turner

Designed by: Paul Cocker

PR: Kerre Chen

Contributors: Faye Bailey, Sarah Koriba, Hannah Keith, Muirne Cunning

Cover art: Luke Prest (www.lukeprest.com)

Published by Meze Publishing Limited
Unit 1b, 2 Kelham Square
Kelham Riverside
Sheffield S3 8SD
Web: www.mezepublishing.co.uk
Telephone: 0114 275 7709
Email: info@mezepublishing.co.uk

Printed by Bell & Bain Ltd, Glasgow

CONTENTS

FOREWORD

Since I opened L'Enclume in Cartmel in 2002, followed by Rogan & Co in 2008, the restaurant industry and food scene as a whole in The Lake District has continued to evolve and has gone from strength to strength. I am so proud to be a part of a group of very talented chefs and businesses here that have contributed to making The Lake District a truly exciting dining destination.

Working in the Lake District, something that came as a real surprise to me is how much I have enjoyed having the space to be able to create my own farm, which we have affectionately named 'Our Farm'. When I first moved up here, I sometimes found it tricky to source specific produce, but Our Farm has allowed us to really work with the seasons and ensure provenance is at the forefront of all that we do.

It started as a bit of a dream project to have my own farm, but thanks to the passion and support of my team and local community, it has grown to be an absolutely integral part of my business, providing produce not only to my restaurants in Cartmel, but also to my recently opened London restaurants, Aulis London and Roganic. It also means that as soon as the produce is ready to harvest, we can put it straight on the menu while it's at its freshest – that in itself feels like a real luxury.

The Lake District has some of the best suppliers and producers in the country and I work hard to build these relationships so that, together with the produce from Our Farm, I can ensure that we are using the best possible ingredients. That way, when it comes to bringing the ingredients into the kitchen you can really celebrate them and let them speak for themselves with their natural flavour. It's this quality that really does impact how each and every dish tastes, and I think that is why the food here is so well respected.

I feel very lucky to spend so much of my time in The Lake District – it is amazing to live and work in a place with such incredible surroundings, which I never tire of!

Simon Rogan – L'Enclume

FOREWORD

I grew up on Cumbria's Irish Sea coast, where I got out and about from an early age, exploring the countryside, hunting and fishing from the off. Without question, my upbringing is the underpinning of my intimate knowledge of both this landscape and environment. I've lived in Cumbria all my life; it's part of who I am and what I'm about.

I've never seen the need to venture away from home. I've done all my training here; I started this incredible culinary journey at Kendal College and then progressed through some of the county's top kitchens, learning all the while. But ultimately it is the knowledge I gained growing up here that plays a major part in my cooking. I know my patch and consequently what grows where and when, information that I see as a vital part of being able to create unique dishes. I've got the whole of Cumbria's bountiful larder to play with… many of my ingredients can be found on the coast, in the gently rolling valleys, the dappled woodland glades, and not forgetting the fells themselves.

We play to our main strength, which is our Lake District location, surrounded by organic farms and heritage livestock. We build relationships with the farmers, and while I guess it might be a cliché to say I'm in my element using the wealth of locally reared and farmed produce in my dishes, it's absolutely true. Our farmers and producers create some of the finest ingredients available anywhere, it's why so many top chefs around the country use Herdwick lamb, Shorthorn beef, Cumbrian venison and Morecambe Bay shrimps, to name just a few.

Using local suppliers and supporting the rural economy is not a marketing gimmick but an obvious choice for me. It's a part of my unwavering drive to extract flavour from the Cumbrian landscape that I believe makes my food so very different, and hopefully means that my menus deliver truly unique taste combinations and a fantastic dining experience.

There's no doubt that cooking is an endless quest for perfection, which is never quite within your grasp. It's something you strive for every day, with every meal, every single dish, every prep; you simply rinse and repeat every day to try and deliver the best you can for your guests.

For me, Cumbria has everything I need. If I can be true to who I am, enjoy creating food from this area's truly amazing produce and share that with others, while nurturing my own family in this place I call home, I'll be a very happy man.

Kevin Tickle - Forest Side

It's pie time
YOU VISITED

The Apple Pie Café and Bakery in Ambleside has been serving up its delicious namesake and plenty of other tasty eatables for over four decades. With a take-out shop, a spacious café and boutique B&B accommodation overlooking the Bridge House, there's something for everyone at this unmissable Cumbrian destination.

Since opening in 1975, The Apple Pie has grown in size and popularity but has remained true to the traditional values at its heart: serving fresh, top-quality products to regular visitors, passing tourists and loyal locals, seven days a week in the heart of the Lake District.

The Ambleside institution is family-run, having been established by Mrs Fielding, as she was always known, and her son David. The next generation has now taken up the rolling pin, first with Simon who was then joined by his brother Richard, though their mum Ann is still in charge of the B&B. The unique accommodation is housed in a listed building which has its own claim to fame; it used to be a solicitor's office belonging to Beatrix Potter's husband.

All of The Apple Pie's products are made on site, with the exception of the sausage rolls, and Cornish pasties (sourced from Cornwall!) The two-storey craft bakery produces cakes, pies and fresh bread made from locally milled flour every day. Perfect picnic foods, along with some lovely gifts and homeware, are available in the take-out shop, and the café offers plenty of seating for all comers to enjoy traditional English delights. The Apple Pie breakfast menu is one of the best in Ambleside; the perfect fuel for heading up into the fells. With a varied lunch menu and options for all dietary requirements, plus a friendly welcome for walkers and dogs alike, it's no wonder that in summer time especially there are queues out the door!

As the name suggests, The Apple Pie is best known for tempting sweet treats, including the hugely popular Bath Buns. These are best sellers – along with the legendary Bramley apple pies, of course – and despite famous competition from down the road, The Apple Pie's gingerbread also has a dedicated following of its own. It's perfect with a pot of Lakeland tea, or locally roasted, barista style coffee to treat yourself.

The hustle and bustle of this lovely Lakeland stone setting makes the café and bakery a must-visit for big groups, families and couples alike. With its celebration of local produce and timeless ways of creating moreish food and sweet treats, The Apple Pie is sure to keep serving hungry customers for years to come.

The Apple Pie
BRAMLEY APPLE PIE

A good apple pie filling has to use Bramley apples, and this unique taste has officially been awarded protected status by the European commission. The reason this particular variety lends itself so well to a fruit pie filling is down to the way the Bramley apple flavour carries right through the cooking process into the finished product. The apple itself cooks to a moist, airy, fluffy texture, which makes the filling almost cream-like. Encased by short pastry that will melt in the mouth, this is a proper English apple pie that will stand out in a crowd!

Preparation time: 20 minutes | Baking time: 40-45 minutes | Serves: 8-10

Ingredients

350g self-raising flour

175g baking margarine (or vegetable shortening for vegan pastry)

80g caster sugar

70ml cold water

2kg (about 4 large) Bramley apples

1 lemon, juiced

225g granulated sugar

Optional filling extras:

100g sultanas

1 level tsp mixed spice

Method

Preheat the oven to 160°c. Rub the self-raising flour and fat together in a large bowl to a course crumb. Next, dissolve the caster sugar in the cold water, and gently combine the sugar solution with the flour and fat until a smooth pastry forms.

Take two thirds of the pastry and, using a little flour for dusting, roll out to approximately 3mm thickness and 38cm in diameter. Lift the pastry using the rolling pin and carefully line a deep 10" pie dish with it. Trim off any excess and add the offcuts to the remaining pastry, then place this and the pastry-lined pie dish into the fridge to chill.

Peel and core the Bramley apples and place in a bowl containing water and the juice of a lemon. Thinly slice the apples, shaking off as much water as possible as you go, and mix with the sugar in a dry bowl.

If using, combine the mixed spice and sultanas and scatter over the pastry base at this stage. Now layer up as much sliced apple as possible in the pie dish.

Roll out the remaining pastry to make a round lid approximately 25cm in diameter and 3mm thick. Wet the edges of the pie dish with a little water and place the lid on the filled pie. Trim off the excess and pinch the edges together with your fingers. Decorate the top with three pastry leaves.

Place the pie into your preheated oven and bake for about 40 minutes, or until the pastry is a lovely golden colour. Remove the pie from the oven when cooked and dust with caster sugar while the pie is still piping hot.

Serve straight away with ice cream or custard, or alternatively you can serve this pie cold with freshly whipped cream.

Cream of
THE CROP

Based in a historic market town which can claim five centuries of recorded cheese-making, Appleby Creamery uses traditional methods from the region to create a variety of award-winning, handmade cheeses in the Eden Valley.

From varying backgrounds within the dairy industry, three born and bred 'Applebians' came together to set up Appleby Creamery. The focus of the venture was to make the most of yields from small traditional dairy herds by creating premium, handmade, artisan cheese that continued the long tradition of cheese-making in the Eden Valley and thus preserved an important part of Cumbrian heritage. Led by expert dairy technologist Maurice Walton, the team gradually built up a range of multi-award-winning cheeses, from regional hard varieties to the soft cheeses, like creamy brie and several goat's and ewe's milk varieties, which they specialise in.

Today, the creamery is run as part of Cows and Co group by Maurice, Mark, Stuart, and Pete, who says that the difference in their backgrounds has proved a real strength for the business. Mark is their "dynamic dairy farmer" whose herd of Ayrshire cows still provides Appleby Creamery with the raw materials for all its cow's milk products. Stuart, an agri-food professional, and Mark go back many years, having done business together previously, and Pete's expertise in sales and marketing has helped to put Appleby and its wonderful cheese-making heritage on the global map.

This might sound like exaggeration, but with a recent win at the World Cheese Awards – where one of the creamery's newest creations, a goat's milk cheese named 'Nanny McBrie', picked up Bronze just months after its launch – the ambitious group are certainly on the up. Plans to expand are already in place, which involve moving premises and extending the product range to include a clotted cream and premium butter just for starters! This won't compromise the artisan nature of the process though; Cumbria's unique food heritage and rural economy are just as integral to the creamery as its location in the heart of the Eden Valley is.

Supporting the local community is hugely important to Appleby Creamery, which it does by nurturing the in-house talent of its apprentices who have all come from within 20 miles or so to learn their trade. Tom Jackson, now head cheese-maker at Appleby Creamery, started as an apprentice himself and has been taught by experts across all aspects of the business. As Stuart points out, "consistency in quality and in the focus behind progress is really where the skill comes in." With five centuries of cheese-making history to draw on, plus the expertise and dedication of a strong team, Appleby Creamery is set to continue moving in a successful and exciting direction.

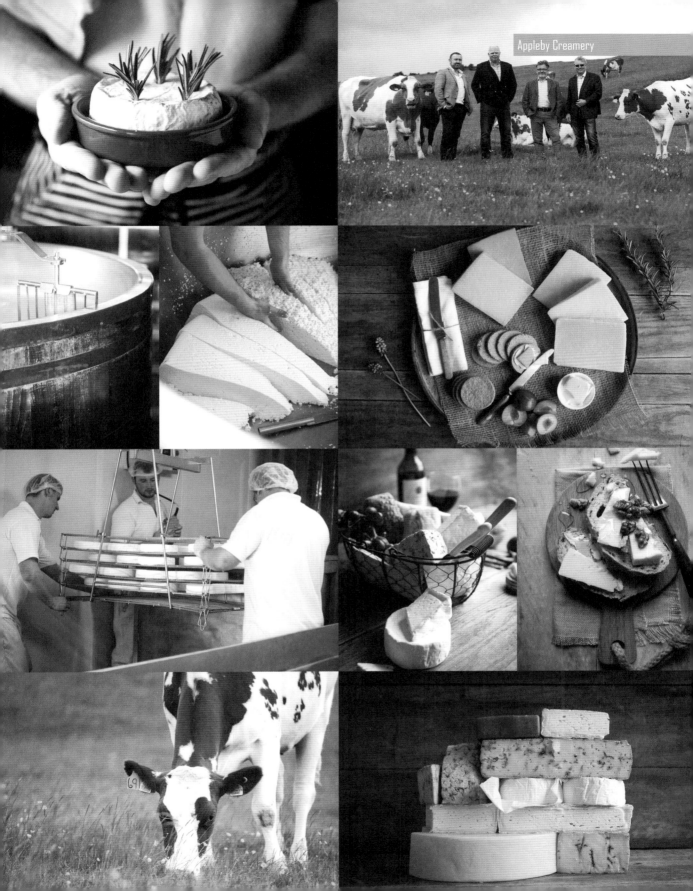

Appleby Creamery

Appleby Creamery
CHICKEN PARCELS
STUFFED WITH SMOKED BRIE

This recipe is one of twelve that Appleby Creamery worked with a development chef to create. Each one uses a particular cheese from the creamery's wonderful range, and together they form a calendar of recipes which everyone can enjoy at home by finding the other eleven online at the creamery website.

Preparation time: 15 minutes | Cooking time: 25 minutes | Serves: 2

Ingredients

2 large chicken breasts, boned and skinless

2 thick slices smoked brie (approx. 50g)

2–4 slices of serrano ham

Salt and cracked black pepper

1 shallot

1 garlic clove

Small bunch of fresh herbs of your choice

Butter, to fry

125ml double cream

Method

Cut a piece out of the centre of the chicken breast to make a pocket. Stuff the chicken breasts with smoked brie. Wrap each in serrano ham and place on a baking tray. Cook on the middle shelf of the oven at 180°c for 20-25 minutes, until the ham has browned and is crisp. Test that the chicken is cooked by putting a skewer into the thickest part of breast. If the juices run clear the chicken is cooked.

Remove the chicken parcels from the cooking tray, and rest them while preparing the sauce. Finely chop a shallot and a clove of garlic with herbs of your choice – parsley, tarragon, marjoram and thyme all work well. Melt a knob of butter in a saucepan and gently fry off the shallot, garlic and herbs. Add the double cream and let the sauce bubble until it thickens. Season to taste.

To serve

For a healthier option serve the chicken parcels with salad. Otherwise, plate up the warm rested chicken parcels and spoon over the sauce. You could serve this version with gently steamed green vegetables and new potatoes.

300 years in THE MAKING

Nestled in the lovely countryside of Lickle Valley, the Blacksmiths Arms is a traditional Lakeland pub with an emphasis on contemporary and local food and drink.

Sophie and Michael bought the Blacksmiths Arms in 2004, having decided they had nothing to lose by upping sticks and trying a change of direction in life. Michael ran restaurants and Sophie worked in TV, but their conflicting hours meant that they were "ships passing in the night" as Sophie puts it. The couple left the flat landscapes of Norfolk for the picturesque (but much wetter) Lakeland fells to run the pub, and – despite Sophie having never pulled a pint before – their joint endeavour paid off so enjoyably that 14 years and two children later, they're still ensuring the warm welcome that the Blacksmiths Arms has extended to all its visitors for nearly 300 years.

One of only two Lake District pubs listed in the CAMRA National Inventory of pubs for interiors of historic significance, the Blacksmiths Arms has its own story to tell too. The building began life as a farmhouse in the 16th century, and by the mid-1700s it had evolved into a blacksmiths and inn. All the beautiful original features – including an oak panelled corridor, range cooker, and slate flooring from local quarries – are still in evidence. Sophie and Michael say that "running the Blacksmiths Arms has a feeling of custodianship…we are merely the current family looking after it for the community's continued benefit".

Today, Michael runs the kitchen with head chef Mark Satterthwaite, who devises menus based on quality produce from local suppliers, and plates the contemporary dishes with an emphasis on beautiful presentation. The Blacksmiths Arms' reputation for a lovely lunch or evening meal, based on the many accolades from returning customers and recognition in well-known publications such as The Good Food Guide and The AA Pub Guide, means booking ahead is definitely advisable! And whether you want to start or finish your meal with a drink or two, the cosy bar with its open fire and sturdy old farmhouse table to gather round is the perfect place to do it. The list of options, from real ales drawn from the three hand-pumps to summer ciders, really celebrates the abundance of great local brewing across Cumbria. Chadwicks' Kirkland Blonde, Barngates' Cracker, Cross Bay's Red IPA, and Pilsner from Tirril Brewery are just some of the varied choices to be found.

After a ramble in the fells or forests of the Lickle Valley walking country, or a day out in the nearest town of Broughton in Furness, the Blacksmiths Arms aims to round off your visit with an experience that's true to Lakeland heritage and culture. The unique beauty of the county, which goes hand in hand with its inviting culinary landscape, was a big part of the draw for Sophie and Michael when they took on the pub, and is something they have no intention of leaving behind!

AS RECOMMENDED IN

THE GOOD
PUB
GUIDE
2018

OUT NOW IN
BOOKSHOPS
AND ONLINE

Visit www.thegoodpubguide.co.uk
to discuss your favourites

Blacksmiths Arms

BRITAIN'S BEST REAL HERITAGE PUBS

IN
RECOGNITION OF
the outstanding historic
importance of parts of its interior

Blacksmiths Arms

is included on CAMRA's
National Inventory of
historic pub interiors

See www.heritagepubs.org.uk
for a full description of this pub.

National Chairman

CAMPAIGN FOR REAL ALE

Blacksmiths Arms

BEETROOT CURED SEA TROUT WITH SPRING GREENS AND SAUTÉED NEW POTATOES

Chef's tips: ensure your fish will lay completely flat in your container before curing. For best results, cure your chosen fish for 48 hours in advance; a 24 hour cure is used in this recipe as a minimum.

Preparation time: 25 minutes, plus 24 hours curing | Cooking time: 1 hour | Serves: 6-8

Ingredients

500g beetroot

300g rock salt (Maldon)

260g caster sugar

170g fresh dill

2 lemons, zested and juiced

1kg side of sea trout (or salmon) pin boned

500g new potatoes, washed

130g unsalted butter

30ml olive oil

300g garden peas

200g broad beans, shelled

10 asparagus spears

Method

For the cure

Peel and roughly chop the beetroot. Blend the beetroot with the salt, sugar, 150g of dill, the lemon zest and juice until smooth and thin.

Line a large container or tray with cling film, leaving plenty of excess over the sides (enough to wrap over the top like a parcel). Pour one third of the beetroot cure into the container and lay the fish, flesh side down, in the cure. Pour over the remaining two thirds of beetroot cure and bring together the excess cling film to create a parcel. Leave the fish in the fridge for a minimum of 24 hours.

For the accompaniments

One hour before you wish to serve the dish, carefully unwrap your fish parcel and rinse off the excess cure under a cold tap.

Leave the new potatoes whole and cook on a rolling boil until soft. Allow to cool, then quarter. Heat a large frying pan with the oil and 100g of butter. Once the butter is bubbling, fry the potato quarters until crisp and golden, then remove from the pan and place on kitchen roll to drain any excess oil.

Remove the base of the asparagus spears, then cut into thirds. Return the frying pan to the heat and fry the peas, beans and asparagus until tender. Remove from the heat and toss in the remaining butter and chopped fresh dill.

To serve

Place the peas and beans across the plate in a Z shape, and add the potato quarters on alternate sides of the greens. Slice the fish into desired portions, then cut each portion diagonally into three. Lay each third of the fish onto the greens and finish by resting your asparagus spears on the fish.

Rocking
THE BOAT

The spectacular views across Windermere Marina are reason enough to visit The Boathouse, but the restaurant, bar and friendly welcome will make sure you'll want to stay and soak up the atmosphere.

Ben Ashworth and Geoff Perrygrove were determined to bring their vision for a relaxed, welcoming bar and restaurant to life at Windermere Marina, and have made The Boathouse busier and better than ever despite some challenging setbacks. The pair's long-held ambition began amidst building works on the marina following severe winter floods, but having battled their way through a stormy start, Ben and Geoff have since enjoyed the company of lots of regular customers and been able to bask in the great reputation they've built up.

Both the bar downstairs and the restaurant upstairs are spacious, and each boast their own unique features but share the same menu, so there's no fear of food envy! The bar welcomes dogs, has a terrace perfect for soaking up elusive summer sunshine, and is Cask Marque accredited: everything you need, in other words, to enjoy a casual drink or meal at any time of day. The restaurant takes bookings – with the window seats overlooking Lake Windermere the first to go – and curates an intimate atmosphere for diners. "The views across the marina are really special, and you feel like you could be anywhere," Ben says of the contemporary, colourful space.

Their building was brand new when The Boathouse opened, and so it had a little more defence against the unpredictable Lakes weather, but was still affected by more severe flooding only two years later. Ben says that the aftermath felt "like going back to year one" but the team set to with determination and a clear idea of their ethos. This includes creating food that is all homemade, locally sourced and using fresh ingredients. The menu is full of hearty favourites from both land and sea, as well as pizza made on site and a wine list to complement the range of international and local flavours.

Ben has lived in the Lakes since he left college, and still uses some of the same suppliers for The Boathouse that he worked with as young chef in others' kitchens. He and Geoff have a wealth of industry experience between them, and play to their strengths to make The Boathouse somewhere for everyone, that's decidedly "not fine dining" but instead focuses on tasty food made well – with a little experimentation from head chef Ben when the menu changes with the seasons. It hasn't all been smooth sailing, but The Boathouse offers a welcome and a taste of the Lakes to treat the eyes and the stomach!

The Boathouse
HAKE, MINTED PEAS AND CHORIZO BUTTER

This dish has been on the menu pretty much since the bar and restaurant's opening, and is so popular that customers will protest if head chef Ben ever takes it off! The 'surf and turf' elements complement not only each other but the enviable location between land and sea too, on the marina just out of Bowness-on-Windermere.

Preparation time: 15 minutes, plus 30 minutes cooling | Cooking time: 35 minutes | Serves: 4

Ingredients

100g cooking chorizo, diced small

2 garlic cloves, finely chopped

½ tsp smoked paprika

100g butter, softened

½ lemon, zest and juice

250g garden peas

75ml double cream

½ a vegetable stock cube

A handful of fresh mint, finely chopped

1 tbsp olive oil

Sea salt

4 x 200g hake portions

Knob of butter

20g watercress, washed and drained

Method

In a dry pan gently fry the chorizo until the oils are released and it smells aromatic. Add one clove of garlic and fry until softened. Add the smoked paprika and fry for another 30 seconds then remove from the heat and allow to cool. When cool mix in the softened butter and lemon. Mix well until all combined.

Bring a pan of water with the garden peas in to a boil, then refresh under cold running water. Place the cream, remaining clove of garlic and stock cube in a small pan and bring to a simmer, then remove from the heat and allow to infuse for 10 minutes. Place the drained peas and cream mixture into a food processor with the mint and pulse until you have a coarse-textured paste.

Heat a non-stick pan with olive oil and a pinch of sea salt until it just starts to smoke. Turn down the heat and add the fish, skin side down, and the knob of butter. Season the flesh of the fish with sea salt and fry for 4-5 minutes until the skin is lovely and golden. Flip the fish over and cook for a further 3-4 minutes until just cooked. Remove from the heat and add a spoonful of chorizo butter on top of each fish skin.

To serve

Reheat the peas gently in a small pan and place in the centre of four dinner bowls or plates. Place the fish under a hot grill to melt the chorizo butter. Place a fish portion on top of the peas and spoon over the chorizo butter. Garnish with the watercress and serve with potatoes of your choice. We serve it with sautéed potatoes.

Something to
SUIT EWE

Set in a hidden corner of this tranquil village, opposite the magnificent medieval Priory, Cartmel Cheeses offers the winning combination of delicious cheese from small batch and artisanal producers, as well as fresh bread, local chutneys and cakes to make this an unmissable Cumbrian destination.

Cartmel Cheeses was established in 2010 by Martin Gott and Ian Robinson to champion Martin's own ewes' milk cheese and add a little extra something to the lovely village of Cartmel, already a fine food destination. In 2015, Martin returned to full-time cheese production and still supplies the shop, and Fran Horne joined Ian in running the business. Peter and Hannah complete the small team at Cartmel Cheeses, and together they are happy to guide customers to the perfect cheese with friendly and knowledgeable advice.

In a purpose-built, temperature-controlled room the cheeses are laid out on a beautiful slate counter, reflecting the landscape of Cumbria with its mountains of cheese. Customers are encouraged to taste before they buy, and the cheeses are cut on a wire to suit. If you're stuck for the perfect accompaniments to your chosen cheeses, the other side of the shop boasts a small deli selling freshly made bread, cakes and local chutneys. Cheeseboards can also be made up and enjoyed in the yard outside, along with a glass of wine or a beer from the neighbours!

Fran and Ian aim to source and buy the best products around; in short, it's got to be good. They work closely with suppliers all over the UK who specialise in mainly raw milk cheeses. Small batch, hand crafted and individual are the most important criteria in their search for fantastic new cheeses, whether they buy from dairy farmers who have begun to diversify, or are approached by artisan cheese-makers with something unique to offer.

If you can't get to the shop, Cartmel Cheeses are at Keswick market every Saturday and also take their market stall to major shows and festivals across the county. Soon customers will be able to purchase their wonderful range of cheeses online, but you are always welcome to taste the cheeses wherever you come across them!

Cartmel Cheeses

Cartmel Cheeses

MRS KIRKHAM'S LANCASHIRE CHEESE AND ONION PIE

"This is the legendary Ruth Kirkham's recipe, using her own raw milk clothbound Lancashire cheese, now made by her son Graham on their farm in Goosnargh, near Preston. When I tested the recipe in Cumbria, there was some consternation that it didn't include potato. I didn't want to change anything, but of course you can decide whether or not potato is your thing!"

Preparation time: 30 minutes | Cooking time: 50 minutes | Serves: 4-6

Ingredients

For the pastry:

165g plain flour

165g self-raising flour

80g lard

80g margarine (we use Stork)

5-6 tbsp cold water

For the filling:

25g butter and a lug of oil, for frying

3 large onions, finely chopped

275g Mrs Kirkham's Lancashire cheese

2 medium eggs, beaten

Salt and pepper

Method

First, make the shortcrust pastry. Put the flour, lard and margarine in a food processor and whizz to form breadcrumbs. Add the water a tablespoon at a time until a dough starts to form. Bring it together gently with your hands to form a ball, place it in a plastic bag and put it in the fridge while you prepare the filling.

Preheat the oven to 200°c or 180°c fan. Heat the butter and oil in a large frying pan, add the onions and soften over a medium heat for around 7 minutes, turning frequently. Try not to let the onions catch; you want them to be soft and translucent. Add some black pepper and put them in a large bowl to cool.

Roll out two thirds of the pastry and line a 20cm diameter x 4cm deep dish (best made in a pie tin so the base doesn't need blind baking). Prick the bottom with a fork.

Crumble the cheese over the onions and add the beaten egg, saving a little to brush over the top of the pie. Stir well, add some salt and more pepper to taste if you wish, then pour the cheese and onion mix into the pie case and spread into an even layer.

Roll out the remainder of the pastry big enough to cover the top of the pie, brush the edge of the pie case with water and press the top on firmly round the edge. Cut off the excess pastry and flute the edges or decorate with a fork. Put a couple of small cuts in the centre of the pie lid, decorate as you wish, and brush with the remaining beaten egg. Cook for around 50 minutes, until the top is firm and golden.

To serve

This delicious pie can be eaten hot or cold (hot is my favourite) so get stuck in!

Get YOUR FIX

Carvetii is a small specialist coffee roaster doing big things in the world of coffee...

Carvetii Coffee is run by coffee connoisseurs Gareth Kemble and Angharad MacDonald, and originated after their self-confessed passion for coffee got a bit out of hand! From roasting green beans in a frying pan while on the hunt for fresh coffee in Cumbria, they now run an exciting, growing business from their roastery in Threlkeld, near Keswick. As specialist coffee roasters, the small team (just four people, including Gareth and Angharad) use an ever-changing selection of high quality coffee beans. They currently supply a string of 4 and 5-star hotels as well as top-end cafes and restaurants, but there is a lot more to the business.

Their coffee is used by the best educators in the industry to train professionals at all levels at the London School of Coffee. At their new, bigger premises there are dedicated workshop spaces where the team go well beyond just selling coffee to their customers. They spend a great deal of time working to educate them on speciality coffee and training them on the equipment as well as providing a full consultancy service including a 24/7 espresso machine repair service. This in turn ensures that the best possible service (and coffee) is delivered to those businesses' own customers and guests. Both Gareth and Angharad are immensely passionate about the speciality coffee industry – Gareth's regular blog has been recognised as one of the 'Top 40 Coffee Blogs For Coffee Enthusiasts' – and their genuine interest, excitement, and in-depth knowledge of all things speciality coffee is abundant as soon as you meet them, and leaves you wanting to learn more.

Having recently secured a contract with one of the world's top espresso machine manufacturers, Carvetii has recently become an approved supplier of Victoria Arduino machines in the North of England and are thrilled to be flying the flag for Cumbria on an international scale. Exciting developments certainly aren't in short supply at the coffee roaster, as the team have plans for further expansion into the building next door in early 2018 and will also be launching their own 'Cumbrian School of Coffee' in 2018 after completing SCA accreditation to offer official SCA qualifications; another Cumbrian first.

Even if you're not lucky enough to be in the area, Carvetii offers an online shop for people to purchase their freshly roasted coffee. This recently branched out to include tea and hot chocolate, which are available on monthly subscriptions. For those interested in creating drinks themselves, Carvetii's workshops are the perfect venue to learn all about being a Home Barista, or even Home Brewing... minus the frying pan of course!

This small speciality coffee roaster is doing big things for coffee-lovers at all levels of knowledge and enthusiasm across Cumbria, the UK and even further afield in the near future; time to wake up and smell the Carvetii coffee!

Carvetii Coffee

Carvetii Coffee
ESPRESSO MARTINI

Created in the 1980s by Dick Bradsel, a London bartender, when a customer asked for a drink that would "wake her up", the original espresso martini combined espresso, vodka, coffee liqueur and sugar.

We think the key to the perfect espresso martini is to use freshly ground beans and an espresso shot pulled over ice. You really want the coffee to cool instantly to prevent oxidisation. Then you need plenty of ice, as this helps to create that beautiful smooth foam layer on the top.

Carvetii is based just across the lake from a local distillery - The Lakes Distillery. We use their 'The Lakes Vodka' which works in harmony with our espresso blend to produce a deliciously stimulating and indulgent espresso martini.

Preparation time: 5 minutes | Serves: 1

Ingredients

Carvetii Espresso Blend pulled over ice (has to chill instantly)

25ml The Lakes Vodka

25ml Kahlua

12ml sugar syrup

1 cocktail cup shaker full of ice (this helps the martini foam)

Method

Once all the ingredients are to hand, shake them vigorously in a cocktail shaker full of ice, pour out through a sieve into a martini glass, and serve to impressed guests!

Garnish with Carvetii coffee beans, if you like.

The ITALIAN DODD

Dodds Restaurant has been a staple of Ambleside for many decades, and during the last it has built up a reputation for a great atmosphere with food and drink that keeps locals coming back for more.

Laszlo and Tamas had dreamt of having their own restaurant since their teenage years, so they felt very lucky to have the opportunity of taking on Dodds Restaurant in 2008 with the support of their previous employer. They felt that the right thing to do was to keep the name, carrying the legacy of the original owner, M.R. Dodds, while bringing the restaurant up to date. This is reflected today in the modern yet cosy dining area and the food served straight from the open kitchen.

They aim for Dodds to stand out from the crowd, as well as to provide a friendly and approachable service thanks to the close-knit team. The menus are filled with wonderful dishes influenced by the flavours of the Mediterranean, and seasonal availability. The focus is on Italian cuisine, as Laszlo – who is head chef – enjoys what he calls the "never ending source of ideas and inspiration" from the wide regional variety it offers. Tamas, who looks after front of house, also likes to experiment in the bar with new drink pairings and he personally chooses the best wines to go with the flavourful food. His team also put a lot of effort into turning locally roasted beans into the smoothest coffee experiences for their guests.

Laszlo often tries out new ideas on the specials menu, as "it's a good way to gauge interest and feedback from the customers." The style of food served at Dodds has led to close relationships with local producers and suppliers, as well as with those across many borders to enable the team to find the best and most unique Italian ingredients and wines. Laszlo sources a wide range of products – from cheese to handcrafted cured meats – from a small supplier based on the island of Sardinia, where every member of the family has a hands-on role!

Laszlo and Tamas agree that "Dodds' biggest accolade is that we have an ever growing customer base and the thumbs up from our happy customers." The two say that it's always nice to look back to their younger selves, who would be going out for a few drinks after a hard day in the restaurant, when they're now running home to see their kids! The duo and their team have worked hard to create a place to eat out that's easy going and a joy to revisit; the bubbly atmosphere filled with the chatter of contented guests is all you need to hear to know they've succeeded!

Dodds Restaurant
SAFFRON SEAFOOD RISOTTO

Dodds' head chef and co-owner Laszlo has chosen to showcase Arborio rice in both of their recipes, as it's such a versatile ingredient and can be used for savoury or sweet dishes.
This fresh seafood risotto evokes memories of sunny holidays by the sea, and is a marriage of Italian cuisine and flavours from The Lakes.

Preparation time: 20 minutes | Cooking time: approx. 1 hour | Serves: 4

Ingredients

1.2 litres chicken stock

2 tbsp butter

1 tbsp olive oil

1 onion, very finely chopped

Pinch of salt

350g Arborio risotto rice

125ml dry white wine, plus a splash for the mussels

½ tsp saffron

20–30 fresh mussels, cleaned

Drizzle of rapeseed oil

4 squid tubes, scored on the inside and cut into strips

20 king prawns, peeled and deveined

Salt and pepper

1 lemon, zested

50g Parmesan

1 tbsp chives, chopped

Pea shoots, to garnish

Extra-virgin olive oil

Method

Heat the stock in a pan over a low heat and have a ladle ready. Melt the butter and olive oil in a high-sided, non-stick pan. Add the onion and a pinch of salt, then cook whilst stirring for 5 minutes until softened but not coloured. Tip in the rice and coat in the oil and butter, cooking for a few minutes until it's beginning to toast.

Pour in the 125ml of wine and cook, stirring, until it has all been absorbed. Add the saffron and begin to add the hot stock, a ladle at a time, stirring continually. Add more stock as it's absorbed, reserving one ladleful for later. After 25-30 minutes, all the stock should be absorbed and the rice should be creamy and al dente.

To prepare the shellfish, steam the mussels in a covered pan with a splash of white wine until all have just about opened. Transfer them into a bowl or a plate straightaway to stop them from over cooking.

Get a very large frying pan very hot, and using a drizzle of rapeseed oil, fry the finely scored squid strips and the peeled, cleaned king pawns until they change colour but are still plump and about halfway done. Scoop the cooked saffron risotto into the frying pan along with a ladleful of chicken stock. Stir everything together, season with salt and pepper, add the steamed mussels and then the Parmesan and the lemon zest. Continue to cook until the mussels are fully opened.

To serve

With an occasional gentle stir, add the chopped chives. Serve with sprigs of pea shoot and a drizzle of extra virgin olive oil. Enjoy with a glass of Pinot Grigio or Soave.

Dodds Restaurant
TORTA DI RISO

This torta di riso is a nice light dessert, perfect for rounding off a wholesome meal.

Preparation time: 20 minutes | Cooking time: approx. 1 ½ hours | Serves: 6

Ingredients

300g Arborio rice

1 litre milk

250g caster sugar

2 vanilla pods

5 whole eggs, separated

Zest of 1 lemon

To serve (optional):

6 tbsp orange marmalade

6 tbsp mascarpone

Icing sugar, to dust

Method

In a thick-bottomed pan cook the Arborio rice with the milk, 100g of the sugar, the lemon zest and one of the vanilla pods (halved and deseeded) until al dente. Set aside to cool down to room temperature.

Beat the five egg whites in a clean, dry mixing bowl with another 100g of sugar until the mixture forms stiff peaks.

Mix the five egg yolks with the remaining 50g of caster sugar until the mixture doubles in size and turns a pale yellow colour.

Very gently, fold half of the egg white mixture and half of the yolk mixture into the cooled cooked rice. Repeat the process until everything is combined, and transfer it to a greased and flour-dusted springform cake tin.

Place the torta di riso into a preheated oven at 190°c for 45 minutes.

To serve

It can be served warm or cold with a dollop of orange marmalade and mascarpone cheese mixed with vanilla seeds on the side. Dust with icing sugar and enjoy with a shot of limoncello!

Land of milk
AND HOGGET

Dodgson Wood is a business with many strings to its bow – fresh and frozen meat from native breeds raised with care and dedication, off-grid accommodation in stunning countryside, a range of beautiful spun wool and even handmade soap all celebrate the bounty of this working farm in sustainable and educational ways.

John Atkinson is the sixth generation to farm the land at Nibthwaite Grange, securing a future for those who come after him and improving on the progress that was made before him. He and his partner Maria Benjamin run the farm along with the help of John's father Bill and eldest son Tom, and believe wholeheartedly in leaving the land in a better state than they found it. This ethos informs everything they do at Dodgson Wood as a specialist in conservation grazing and a business, comprising fresh and frozen meat from the animals they raise on the farm, a range of spun wool and handmade soap, and unique off-grid accommodation and camping.

Dodgson Wood is committed to providing great quality produce at affordable prices, and does this by cutting out the middle man, instead selling directly to local restaurants such as the Old Stamp House in Ambleside as well as to private customers. John and Maria raise a large flock of Cheviot sheep on Nibthwaite Grange Farm for their wool and meat, as well as a smaller number of rare breed Castlemilk Moorits and Teeswaters. They also have a Jersey cow whose milk is the base product for Maria's expanding range of handmade soap, a growing herd of Luing cattle (a hardy Scottish breed) and a small herd of Whitebred Shorthorns, a native regional breed which is now rare. With welfare at the centre of their concerns, they are involved at every stage of the process and

work with a local abattoir and a local butcher where they can guarantee good practice.

All fresh and frozen meat can be couriered in chilled boxes, and is expertly portioned into smaller cuts ideal for home cooking after being hung for at least a week at the butchers. Both the mutton and hogget from Dodgson Wood is extremely tender, and Maria explains that customers are often blown away to discover how much flavour and delicacy the meat has, and once they've had their first try they nearly always come back for more! Individuals can buy products from the Dodgson Wood website or from the farm itself, whether they're passing by or staying in the eco-friendly barn, campsite or cottage on the farmland.

You can truly retreat from modern living in the off-grid accommodation at Dodgson Wood, but the business' owners have also found ways to embrace the somewhat uncertain future of British farming by diversifying and protecting the land they work with. Being prepared and self-reliant is as important to John and Maria as working with organisations like the National Trust, Hay Bridge Nature Reserve and Friends of the Lake District to conserve the very special environment in which they make their home and their living.

Dodgson Wood
MARIA'S MUTTON KOFTAS

Our Cheviot sheep graze the fells around Parkamoor, an off-grid 16th century cottage we look after and rent out to visitors. This recipe was developed with our guests in mind. As there is no oven, just a small hob for cooking on, and the nearest shop is five miles away, I wanted to create a delicious meal that, except the fresh mutton which can be bought from our farm, relies on store cupboard ingredients. I love Middle Eastern flavours, so I like to add sumac, a lovely tangy spice, to these koftas. If you don't have any, they are just as delicious without it, or with an alternative spice like paprika.

Preparation time: 15 minutes | Cooking time: 50 minutes | Serves: 4

Ingredients

500g minced mutton (or lamb if you can't get mutton)

1 tsp sumac

¼ tsp cinnamon

1 tsp cumin

¼ tsp crushed chillies

1 tbsp treacle

½ tsp salt

¼ tsp pepper

400g passata (or a tin of tomatoes)

Method

In a bowl, combine all the ingredients except the passata and mix thoroughly. Your hands are the best tool for this.

Make a small patty, and fry it off so you can check the flavours and adjust as necessary.

When the flavours are right, form the rest of the spiced mince into golf ball-sized koftas and fry them, draining off the fat as you go.

Once the koftas are lightly browned, add the passata or tinned chopped tomatoes.

Let this simmer until the tomato sauce has reduced to a nice thick consistency. It should take around 30 minutes, by which time the sauce will be bursting with flavour from the koftas.

Serve this with warm flatbreads, rice or couscous for a delicious Middle Eastern-inspired meal.

A room with A VIEW

Situated within Lakeland's flagship store in Windermere, First Floor Café is an ideal spot for locals, shoppers and visitors to take in stunning views while enjoying coffee and cake, a light lunch or a delicious meal from the revitalised menu created by chefs who have worked at some of the best restaurants in Cumbria.

There has been a café serving locals and visitors to Lakeland's flagship store for over 30 years and, in more recent times, it moved to the renowned kitchenware chain's first floor – hence the name First Floor Café. Long associated with great talent within the food world, the current chefs and owner took over the business, which is independent from Lakeland itself, in 2017, and have since spruced up the menu. Customer favourites, such as the classic sausage and mash or omelette Arnold Bennett haven't gone anywhere though – and First Floor's customers know what they like, as some have been visiting weekly or even daily since the café opened!

It's not only the customers who have stuck around; many of the staff members are just as dedicated and on first-name terms with the regulars, lending an especially welcoming atmosphere to the large and airy space. The café can see up to 500 people visit in a day, and provides table service all year round. With influences ranging from the very Cumbrian to the exotic, the menu takes current food trends, dietary requirements and traditional tastes in its stride.

Much of the produce used in the café kitchen is local, as First Floor Café uses nearby suppliers who update the chefs daily to let them know what's in season so it can take pride of place on the specials board. Top-quality meat from family butchers in Staveley and Grange sits comfortably alongside Cartmel Valley game and fish from Fleetwood Docks. Or if it's coffee and cake that you're in need of after a hard day's shopping, then First Floor Café is the place to enjoy locally blended coffee and freshly baked treats to get your mouth watering.

If an authentic taste of the Lakes isn't quite enough to satisfy, you can also feast your eyes on the incredible views through First Floor Café's panoramic windows. The lake, mountains and fells provide an impressive backdrop in any weather, and make First Floor Café a truly special place to enjoy the Lake District in comfort and great taste!

First Floor Café

First Floor Café
FISH CHOWDER

The chefs at First Floor Café have a lot of creative licence, as the menu aims to cater for a wide range of customers and offer lots of choice, from the traditional to something a little more unusual. This chowder is a real classic.

Preparation time: 20 minutes | Cooking time: approx. 45 minutes | Serves: 6

Ingredients

450g smoked haddock

300g salmon

580ml milk

2 tbsp vegetable oil

50g butter

3 sticks of celery, finely sliced

2 medium onions, finely sliced

1 head of fennel, finely sliced

1 garlic clove

175ml white wine

2 large potatoes, peeled and sliced

600ml vegetable stock

200g leeks, finely sliced

140g sweetcorn kernels

600g new potatoes, cooked and sliced

Chervil and chives, finely chopped

Salt and pepper

Method

Take the skin off the haddock and the salmon, keeping the haddock skin to one side. Cut the fish into evenly-sized pieces. In a saucepan, bring the milk up to a simmer and place the haddock skin in it to infuse. Turn off the heat and leave to cool, then take the haddock skin out of the milk. Keep the milk for later.

Heat up the oil and butter in a deep saucepan. Fry the celery, onions, fennel and garlic on a high heat until soft but not coloured. Add the wine, the sliced potatoes and stock and bring to the boil. Reduce the heat to a simmer for 10 minutes until the vegetables have softened, add the infused milk, then blend with a hand blender until smooth.

Put the pan back onto a low heat and add the leeks, sweetcorn and new potatoes. Simmer for 5 minutes then add the diced fish and simmer for a further 5 minutes, or until the fish is just starting to flake.

To serve

Adjust the seasoning if needed, then stir through the chopped chervil and chives. Serve in warm bowls with fresh crusty bread, if you like, though this chowder is a lovely hearty meal on its own!

Something old,
SOMETHING NEW

Set in the midst of the Grasmere countryside, Forest Side is both a retreat into Lakeland luxury and a celebration of the landscape that is fundamental to everything from its interior to the food and drink created and served there.

Grasmere was described by William Wordsworth as "the loveliest spot that man hath ever found". The team at Forest Side certainly agree, having taken on the renovation of a 150-year-old building to create a luxurious retreat surrounded by stunning landscapes, comprising a Michelin-starred restaurant and twenty luxurious bedrooms, not to mention the acres of grounds and gardens full of native flora and fauna to be used throughout the hotel.

The team at Forest Side are passionate about food and provenance, and nowhere is this more apparent than in the restaurant run by head chef Kevin Tickle. The food that Kevin creates with his team at Forest Side is inspired by the landscape in which it sits, and uses the bountiful larder of the Cumbrian countryside to reflect this. The emphasis on local produce means that 90% of ingredients are sourced within 10 miles of the restaurant, and much of them actually come from Forest Side's own kitchen garden, as well as Kevin's foraging trips into the fields, coastline and forests he's known since childhood. Seasonality plays a large part, so for Kevin working with local suppliers and therefore supporting the rural economy is just common sense. He also uses the ancient techniques of preserving, pickling and curing great

ingredients for use during the leaner months; a highlight has to be the range of charcuterie developed in-house with his sous chef Martin Frickel.

Forest Side is committed to ensuring that guests have the very best experience possible, and this ethos extends to every aspect of the restored former gentleman's residence. It took real passion to see the property's potential through the dilapidation and overgrowth, and to then undertake its rejuvenation with such careful attention to detail. Having revealed some wonderful original features, the renovation emphasised the former luxury of the gothic mansion with an approach that cut no corners. From specially made Westmorland beds to deep-pile Herdwick wool carpets (that required the largest order for Herdwick fleece ever placed with Wools of Cumbria!) the rooms are appointed with top quality furnishings and designed by James Mackie with the hotel's unique setting always in mind.

Whether you plump for a mid-week getaway or a weekend away from it all, you can be sure of a dining experience to remember. Forest Side has lovingly married both the old and the new, to offer a place that resonates with the beauty of the Lake District in its food, drink, décor and inspiration.

Forest Side
MUSHROOM BROTH
AND MUSHROOM RAGU

If you can't get wild mushrooms for this recipe, chestnut mushrooms are a great alternative. Beef marrow bones work best in the mushroom ragu, which is delicious served with beef brisket.

Preparation time: 20 minutes, plus 5 days for brining | Cooking time: approx. 2 ½ hours | Serves: 4

Ingredients

For the mushroom broth:

200g wild mushrooms (girolles, chanterelles or grey oysters)

1 shallot

2 garlic cloves

100ml Madeira

1 litre vegetable stock

50g dried mushrooms

For the pickled shimejis:

1 punnet shimeji mushrooms

200ml pickling vinegars

For the mushroom ragu:

100g bone marrow (preferably beef)

200g wild mushrooms

1 shallot, finely diced

1 garlic clove

Chopped chives

Method

For the mushroom broth

Sweat the wild mushrooms, shallot and garlic. Add the Madeira and reduce the liquid by half, and then add the vegetable stock and dried mushrooms. Simmer the broth for 1 hour and then strain through a fine sieve.

For the pickled shimejis

Bring the 200ml of pickling vinegars to the boil. Pour the boiling vinegar over the shimejis and set aside for at least 30 minutes.

For the mushroom ragu

Firstly, you will need to smoke the beef bones (ask your butcher for inch long pieces). You can smoke them in a large lidded pan if you don't own a smoker. Simply scatter some smoking chips into the pan and put on a high heat until the chips start to smoke heavily. Place a small cooling rack inside the pan, then place the bone marrow into a deep sided tray and place on top of the rack. Place the lid on the pan and then tightly tin foil the lid to seal it. Remove from the heat and set aside for 2 hours to continue smoking.

Remove the smoked bones from the pan and remove the marrow. Then gently fry on a low heat to render out the fat, which should take 20-30 minutes. Then pass the rendered marrow through a fine sieve. After this, simply sweat the mushrooms, shallots and garlic in the bone marrow for 3-4 minutes on a low heat, allowing the mushrooms to absorb as much bone marrow as possible.

To serve

Place the wild mushrooms in a bowl and sprinkle a few pickled shimejis over the top. Reheat the mushroom ragu and finish with some chopped chives. Then add a teaspoon of the mix to the bowl containing the shimejis. The broth can then either be poured over the contents of the bowl or served separately as a sipping broth.

Forest Side
LEMON SOLE, CELERIAC, MUSSELS AND SAVOURY

Ideally buy fresh sustainably sourced fish from your local fishmonger where you can. Lemon sole has a sweet, delicate flesh that suits a huge range of recipes. Widely available, they're a tasty alternative to Dover sole and easier on the pocket for those on a tighter budget.

Preparation time: 45 minutes | Cooking time: approx. 2 hours | Serves: 4

Ingredients

2 celeriac

1 litre vegetable stock

2 shallots, finely chopped

2 garlic cloves, crushed

50g unsalted butter

300g winter savoury

1 litre sunflower oil

4 x 100g lemon sole fillets

1 litre water

200g butter

Salt, to taste

200g large mussels

1 punnet shimeji mushrooms

Pinch of celery cress

Method

Start by peeling the celeriac, and then cut one into quarters and the other into 1cm cubes. Roast the 1cm cubes at 180°c until golden and set aside. Poach the quarters in the vegetable stock until cooked through, tear into 1cm shards and reserve both the stock and the shards.

Place the roasted celeriac cubes into the reserved vegetable stock along with the chopped shallots and the garlic. Bring to the boil and then simmer for one hour. Pass the sauce through a sieve and then whisk in the butter and season.

Blanch the savoury in boiling water, refresh in iced water, and then blitz in a blender with the sunflower oil until smooth. Pass the flavoured oil through a piece of muslin and cool in the fridge.

Score a line across each sole halfway down the fillet so that you can fold them in half to create a thicker piece. Fry the fish in a pan until golden in colour, then flip each fillet over and finish with foamy butter off the heat. Make a butter emulsion by whisking the water, butter and salt together. Reheat the roasted celeriac in this, then add the cleaned mussels and shimeji mushroom caps 1 minute before you are ready to serve.

To serve

Remove all the components from their various cooking vessels and place on a drainage tray. Remove the mussels from their shells. Place the fish on the plate, then the celeriac cubes and shards and the mussels. Sprinkle the shimejis on top. Add the celeriac sauce and drizzle the savoury oil over it. Finish the dish with a pinch of celery cress.

What a CATCH

A tempting combination of modern fishmonger, diverse seafood deli and innovative sushi maker, Fyne Fish is a business on a mission to bring quality fresh marine produce to Cumbria.

Fyne Fish opened its doors in November 2011 in Cockermouth, the quaint town famed for being the birthplace of William Wordsworth, as well as being known in the Lake District for its array of independent shops and businesses. The fishmonger's is also a seafood deli and sushi-lovers paradise, owned and operated by husband and wife team John and Sharon Heron. The couple were inspired to start their venture by the lack of quality fresh fish available in the area, and have since made waves as finalists in both the Best Newcomer and Food Innovation categories of the 2015 Cumbria Life awards, as well as winner of the Best Specialist Retailer.

It's a fishmonger's with a difference, following traditional values yet employing a modern approach to provide the locals (and not-so-locals) with a vast array of fresh fish and seafood, sourced where possible from the Cumbrian coast, as well as national and international waters. The wet fish counter can often boast more than forty different species of fresh fish and seafood, ranging from traditional cod, salmon and haddock to the more exotic red snapper, marlin, swordfish and shark, or even geoduck clams, soft shell crab and fresh seaweeds. The seafood deli offers a huge selection of ready-to-eat seafood, including Solway Brown shrimps, dressed local

lobster or Whitby crab, and Arbroath smokies, as well as their own shop-made pâtés, fish pies, luxury seafood terrines and bespoke seafood platters to meet any taste or budget.

What makes Fyne Fish really stand out, however, is their fusion-style menu of fresh sushi and sashimi, which is prepared onsite every Friday and Saturday morning. Over the last five years, Sharon and John have got this down to such a fine art that their sushi has been described more than once as the best-tasting sushi in the world! They also run a Sushi School, teaching people from all over Cumbria and beyond on extremely popular day courses throughout the year.

The passion that John, Sharon and their staff feel for the business and the products they create really shines through. The team are full of recipe suggestions and new ideas for customers to try; the hardest part about a visit to Fyne Fish is often getting back out the door! The combination of the day's freshly delivered catch and such friendly, efficient service draws customers from miles around to both the Cockermouth shop and the pop-ups at Keswick market, local shows and food festivals all year round. Simply put, the clue's in the name; fine fish is what these people are all about!

Fyne Fish

Fyne Fish
AN INDULGENT FISH PIE

A fish pie can be as indulgent as you wish. It can be made with a mixture of white fish (cod, haddock, pollock or hake) with added smoked fish or prawns, or you can go the whole hog and use luxury cuts of halibut, monkfish or tuna! Cream can be substituted with a lighter crème fraîche, or you can make your own roux for a white sauce.

Preparation time: 20 minutes | Cooking time: 1 hour 15 minutes | Serves: 4

Ingredients

1.5kg potatoes

2 tbsp olive oil

300ml fresh cream

40g butter

750g mixed fish fillets, skinned and boned (the choice of fish is yours entirely)

1 medium leek

1 carrot

1 tsp wholegrain mustard

2 handfuls of fresh spinach

Bunch of fresh parsley

½ lemon, juiced

Salt and pepper

To serve:

Broccoli, asparagus or green beans

Method

Preheat the oven to 180°c. Peel and cut the potatoes into small, even pieces and then boil in salted water until tender. Strain the potatoes and add a tablespoon of olive oil, 50ml of fresh cream, and 15g of butter. Mash until soft and creamy. Cut the fish into evenly sized chunks and set aside.

Thinly slice the leek and grate the carrot. Melt the remaining butter with the olive oil in a pan, add the vegetables and fry for approximately 5 minutes, without allowing them to colour. Once the leek and carrot are soft, add the remainder of the cream, allow everything to come to the boil, add the mustard and season to taste. Stir to combine. Add the spinach, reduce the heat accordingly, and stir the spinach through, which will wilt immediately. Add the fish, chopped parsley and lemon juice and double check the seasoning.

Transfer the fish mix to an ovenproof dish, and carefully top with the creamy mash potato. Place the fish pie on an oven tray (in case it bubbles over) and place the tray on the middle shelf of the preheated oven for 10-15 minutes. Brown under the grill if needed.

If you have made the pie ahead of time and are cooking it from cold, the cooking time should be increased to 30-40 minutes.

Decorate the cooked pie with parsley stems, and serve with freshly cooked broccoli, asparagus or green beans.

Hops, barrel AND SOUL

Full of flavour, handcrafted, bold and personal; these qualities fit both the beer and the approach to brewing it that the team at Hawkshead Brewery create.

Hawkshead Brewery has been creating its modern, innovative and distinctive range of beers since 2002 under the direction of beer connoisseur Alex Brodie. His small team began their endeavours in a barn just outside the village of Hawkshead, but quickly outgrew it and moved to their current site in Staveley beside the River Kent, joining other small artisanal producers in the Mill Yard amid beautiful countryside. They've gone from producing 30 barrels in a week to 220 barrels, but continue to brew mostly cask beers in the Great British tradition, as well as lagers and other keg beers.

The range includes thirst quenching session beers, big hopped modern pale ales, deep dark stout, sours and a core range of cask beers, all of which have scooped an impressive number of awards between them from diverse bodies such as Great Taste, CAMRA and Cumbria Life. Recipe development comes under the remit of head brewer Matt Clarke, who proudly represents his home turf with plenty of New Zealand hoppy blends, alongside eclectic inventions inspired by current trends and perfected in small batches. Tonka bean, tiramisu and chuckleberry (not all together!) are just a few recent examples of unusual flavours which have embodied the ethos of experimentation, excitement and collaboration at Hawkshead Brewery.

The brewing process is labour intensive and hands-on for the five brewers, and has even included visits to hop farmers across the UK, the US, New Zealand and Slovenia. As the team themselves put it, Hawkshead Brewery is small enough to have fun, but big enough to deliver great beer to people who love it on a daily basis. You can even taste the end product right where it's brewed, as expansions back in 2010 allowed the brewery to open its own tap in the building next door. Long tables, sofas, and a bar complete with casks, kegs, bottles and cans of the good stuff make The Beer Hall an ideal spot to enjoy a drink, and a nosey into the workings of the brewery itself through the large surrounding windows.

The huge success of this small independent speaks volumes about the passion, depth of knowledge and commitment to great beer that unites the close-knit team at Hawkshead Brewery. They make the kind of beer they love to drink, and don't compromise on either flavour or ambition! In the near future, the team will be running two brew kits, using their original for small batch experimentation and development, and a second on another site which will be the very first of its kind in the UK, putting the Lake District right at the cutting edge of the British beer renaissance.

Hawkshead Brewery
BEER AND ONION SOUP

This take on a classic dish sums up our cooking style in a nutshell. Simple and rustic, but done properly and packed with flavour. We make our own stock from scratch and use the beer we brew on-site to full effect.

Preparation time: 15 minutes | Cooking time: 45 minutes | Serves: 6

Ingredients

60g butter

750g white onions

1–2 tsp salt

30g plain flour

200ml Hawkshead Brewery Dry Stone Stout

1 litre beef stock

1–2 tsp cracked black pepper

1 tbsp dark soy sauce (optional)

Sourdough bread (roughly 1 slice per portion)

Mature cheddar, grated (allow up to 50g per portion)

Method

First, prepare the ingredients. Grate the cheddar and peel, halve and thinly slice the onions. Cut the bread into roughly centimetre squares and remove the crusts if you like, then lightly toast on both sides.

Melt half of the butter in a large pan, then add the onions along with a teaspoon of salt and cook on a high heat for around 10 minutes until soft and juicy but not browned. Then remove the onions from the pan and set aside.

In the same pan, melt the rest of the butter, then add the flour and stir on a medium heat with a wooden spoon for 1-2 minutes until completely combined to a bubbling paste. Pour in the beer, stir vigorously and cook until the mixture thickens and you start to see a few bubbles again. (Take care as this stage can create a lot of steam and spitting! If the mixture is too hot, just slide the pan off the heat until it settles down.)

Add the onions back into the pan along with the beef stock. Bring to the boil and simmer for 5-10 minutes. Add more salt and pepper to taste, and depending on the quality of the beef stock you may wish to add a tiny pinch of sugar. This recipe works best when well-seasoned with a good 'bite' of pepper so don't be shy with it! For extra depth of flavour and colour add the soy sauce at this stage.

To serve

Place six heatproof serving bowls onto a baking tray and briefly warm them under the grill, then ladle in the soup till the bowls are about three quarters full. Top with the sourdough croutons and plenty of cheese, then put back under the grill until melted and bubbling. Take care when handling as the bowls and contents will be extremely hot by now, then get stuck in!

Embellish with RELISH

On finding themselves in a bit of a pickle, café owners Mark and Maria decided to embark on a new culinary adventure that has preserved a great Cumbrian tradition and brought relish to condiment-lovers across the county and beyond...

Hawkshead Relish Company began life in the kitchen of a café, run by Mark and Maria Whitehead, that served local food in the historic village of Hawkshead. When the couple struggled to find condiments good enough to complement the tasty meats, cheeses and other home-grown delights they had on their café menu, the obvious solution was to start creating their own. Mark already had a keen interest in food history as well as a knack for discovering great flavour combinations, so one of the first products put up for taste-testing in the café was a Westmorland Chutney, full of the dried fruits and spices that would have originally been imported into the region via merchant trade.

More chutneys, pickles and relishes followed, which went down so well with customers that they had to have a jar or two to take home as well! Things went from strength to strength until the outbreak of foot-and-mouth brought everything to halt for Cumbria. They were "convinced that would be the end of it" as Maria says, but the pair weren't going to give in without a fight. They proposed to set up as a wholesale producer; the bank saw the potential and gave them a financial lifeline and the rest, as they say, is history!

Several years down the line, the café is now a shop where you can try and buy from the vast range of Hawkshead Relish Company's products. Production – at around 25 tonnes per month – has moved to a beautiful 16th century barn with a shiny new kitchen and a team of 28 local condiment enthusiasts. Maria describes the business as a "family network" because the team, including her own daughters and brother, are a close knit bunch, looking after each other while having a few giggles together too.

The only difference between the recipes used at Hawkshead Relish Company and those you could use in your own home is scale. All the chutneys, jams, pickles, relish and sauces are made in traditional open pans and "simple, fresh and authentic" flavours are paramount. Innovative, forward-looking and committed to bolstering the local economy as well as their own exciting future developments, Hawkshead Relish Company has made a true success of Mark and Maria's enduring passion for what they do.

Hawkshead Relish Company

Hawkshead Relish
RED CHICKEN CURRY

Most 'Indian' restaurants in Britain are actually run by Bangladeshis, and the most revered town for food in Bangladesh is Sylhet. This recipe originates in Sylhet, but interestingly uses bright red Kashmiri chilli powder, chilli jam and tomato to give it the distinctive bright red colour. If you wish to make it hotter, just add more chilli powder or Hawkshead Relish Chilli Jam!

Preparation time: 20 minutes | Cooking time: approx. 45 minutes | Serves: 4

Ingredients

Piece of fresh ginger (approx. 3 x 1 cm), peeled

3 heaped tsp Hawkshead Relish Hot Garlic Pickle

2 large very ripe tomatoes, or 1 x 400g tin chopped tomatoes

1 tbsp tomato purée

1 tsp cumin seeds

4 tbsp sunflower or rapeseed oil

350g red or white onions, chopped

2 tsp bright red or Kashmiri chilli powder

160ml water

3 tsp ground coriander

½ tsp ground turmeric

1 tsp garam masala

900g chicken thighs, skinned

1 tsp salt

2 tsp Hawkshead Relish Chilli Jam

750ml chicken stock

2 tsp white wine vinegar

1 tsp sugar (only if using tinned tomatoes)

Method

Roughly chop the ginger and put into a blender with the Hawkshead Relish Hot Garlic Pickle, tomatoes, tomato purée and cumin seeds. Blend well and set aside.

Heat the oil in a wide pan and fry the onions until lightly coloured. Add the chilli powder, quickly followed by 150ml of water, stir and bring to the boil. Add the coriander and turmeric and stir well. Add the garam masala and the remaining 10ml of water. Cook for 1 minute.

Add the chicken and a teaspoon of salt. Fry the chicken in the spices, stirring continuously so that the chicken is coated in the spice mix, ensuring that the ingredients do not stick to the pan.

After about 3-5 minutes, add the blended ginger, garlic and tomato mixture and the Hawkshead Relish Chilli Jam. Stir well. Add the chicken stock, bring to the boil, then simmer for 20 minutes, or until the chicken is cooked.

Taste to check the salt level, then add the vinegar (and sugar if using), and cook for 1 minute.

To serve

Serve with Bombay potatoes (or rice and naan bread), Hawkshead Relish Mango Chutney and an ice cold glass of Hawkshead Brewery Lakeland Lager.

Simply
THE BEST

Higginsons of Grange pride themselves on sourcing the best quality produce from local farms and suppliers, available to customers from their double-fronted butchers and deli in Grange-over-Sands.

The Higginsons story began in 1983 when Stuart and Pauline returned to Grange-over-Sands from Australia, where they had met while working as a butcher and a chef respectively, to set up home and a business in Stuart's home town. Fast-forward thirty five years and the business has become one of the best regarded independent butchers and pie makers in the country. Perfectly placed in the Edwardian coastal town, the business reflects the culinary delights of Cumbria's coast and fells, selling fresh local meats, sausages and bacon cured on the premises, as well as cheeses, ready meals and much more.

Stuart has reared his own free-range pork and lamb for many years, and his longstanding passion for top quality produce has inspired the simple ethos behind Higginsons of Grange, which is to go the extra mile in order to source and prepare the very best for customers to enjoy. Actual food miles, on the other hand, are kept to a minimum by working with local farmers who provide the vast majority of the meat sold on site. When it comes to the butchery and preparation, traditional techniques and methods are practiced by an expert team, led by senior butcher Mark who has over 30 years at Higginsons to his name. Regional specialities such as Lakeland Herdwick lamb and Morecambe Bay Saltmarsh lamb are particular seasonal highlights. Trusted supplier relationships mean that all of Higginsons' products have excellent traceability,

so important to today's customers, some of whom have been known to travel over 100 miles just to stock up!

Countless awards over the years have rewarded the hard work that the Higginson family and their staff have put into maintaining excellence, not least the reader-nominated Lifetime Achievement Award at Cumbria Life Food & Drink Awards in 2016 and a trio of golds from the 2017 Smithfield Awards, run by the Q Guild of Independent Butchers. There's always a queue winding out of the take-out shop or the butchers and delicatessen – quality speaks for itself, and with online ordering now available, Higginsons of Grange are known to loyal (and even royal) customers across the UK. They regularly attend county shows too, one of which was visited by Prince Charles who was impressed enough to purchase some sausages from their stall!

Whatever the occasion, Higginsons of Grange aim to provide the best, offering bespoke options such as tiered wedding pies and Christmas boxes full of all the trimmings. Their dedication to quality is second to none, and those with a similar passion for traceable, local and most importantly delicious food will delight in the treasure trove they curate.

HIGGINSONS
of GRANGE

AWARD
WINNING
BUTCHERS

ESTABLISHED
1983

VOTED
BRITAINS
BEST
BUTCHERS

Higginsons of Grange

HIGGINSONS' CUMBERLAND COIL WITH GRAINY MUSTARD MASH & ROOT VEGETABLES

Higginsons' award-winning Cumberland sausage has a delicate spiced flavour and is perfect accompanied by a mustard mash and some buttery seasonal root vegetables – parsnips, squash or any similar alternative work just as well as carrots – and making your own onion gravy is well worth the extra few minutes to finish the dish. This is classic comfort food and an easy supper – enjoy!

Preparation time: 10 minutes | Cooking time: 30 minutes | Serves: 2

Ingredients

1 Cumberland coil (approx. 450g)

450g Maris Piper potatoes

1 tsp wholegrain mustard

Knob of butter

Salt and pepper, to taste

Handful of Chantenay carrots (or alternative)

Pinch of sugar

For the gravy (optional):

300ml gravy base, or 1 good quality stock cube

1 large white onion

Knob of butter

1 tsp cornflour

Salt and pepper, to taste

Method

Place the sausage under a low-medium grill (don't prick the skin). As soon as one side starts to brown, turn the sausage over and grill the other side. Repeat until the sausage is golden brown on all sides and piping hot; approximately 25 minutes. Leave to cool slightly before serving.

While the sausage is grilling, keep a close eye on it and prepare the mash. Peel and chop the potatoes into medium-sized pieces and place into a pan of cold, salted water. Bring to the boil and cook until the potatoes are tender; 15-20 minutes. Strain the potatoes then add a knob of butter and season. Mash the potatoes until smooth and creamy, then add the wholegrain mustard and mix well.

For the carrots, peel if necessary and remove ends. Place into a pan of cold, salted water and bring to the boil. Cook until tender then strain and add a knob of butter to the pan along with a pinch of sugar. Turn the carrots gently in the pan until they are glossy.

To finish off the recipe with a quick, homemade onion gravy, halve and thinly slice the onion and sauté in a heavy-based pan with a knob of butter until soft. Make up the stock or gravy base and add to the pan. Bring slowly to the boil. Mix a teaspoon of cornflour with a little warm water until smooth, then add this to the gravy, stirring until thoroughly mixed. Allow to thicken and season.

To serve

Place the vegetables next to a generous spoonful of the mustard mash, top with the Cumberland Coil, and add a ladleful of hot onion gravy if including. Enjoy on a wintery evening by a roaring fire.

Tapas to transport YOU

Come rain or shine, L'al Churrasco is the place to go for a taste of
Mediterranean tapas in Cumbria.

L'al Churrasco brings something a little different to the South Furness area. With a constantly changing menu full of tempting, freshly made food and a 'tapas taster' option allowing customers to pick and mix any dishes they like, bespoke dining experiences are the order of the day. The unusual name hints at the dual nationality of the Ulverston restaurant; l'al means little in Cumbrian dialect, and churrasco means charcoal grill in Portuguese. "I think it took about a year before the local people could pronounce it correctly, with us often being referred to as the 'tapas place up the road'" says chef patron Harrison Albion.

That's Spanish, Portuguese and Southern Mediterranean tapas to be specific, which uses ingredients that originate from around the world and fine dining techniques to elevate ordinary dishes to those that completely wow customers. As Harry puts it though, "food doesn't need to be complicated to be special", so the tapas is simple in design and often uses just three to five ingredients, expertly matched with spices for bold flavours and winning combinations.

There are certain dishes that L'al Churrasco daren't take off the menu, such is their popularity, like the halloumi and the pork belly. To keep things fresh, the small but mighty kitchen team modify the accompaniments instead, according to the season. Harry is extremely proud of the restaurant's commitment to sourcing locally and ethically. He works with suppliers who can share their expertise and offer inspiration, including Brocklebanks (just three doors up) for the colourful shelves of vegetables, local butchers Irvings for the tastiest lesser-known cuts of meat, and seafood from Morecambe Bay.

The restaurant's commitment to freshly made food to please all taste buds is matched by its warm, open dining space to please all visitors. The interior combines decorative touches in Moorish style with industrial finishes – such as a 'rusty' wall, in the naturally pleasing tones of oxidised iron mixed into the plaster – that gives L'al Churrasco a completely individual feel and look. Everything from the service to the mural done by a friend focuses on the personable experience Harry and his team want to provide for each customer. For casual eating out with a twist, L'al Churrasco has all the warmth and welcome you could wish for!

L'al Churrasco

CHURRASCO SPECIALS

L'al Churrasco
AIOLI

This aioli is a firm favourite on our menu – and for good reason too! We serve ours with calamari but it's a very versatile accompaniment and can be used for many things: as a topping for grilled white fish; with roasted summer vegetables; a side for omelettes; or even as an upscale bread dip.

Preparation time: 10 minutes | Serves: 10-12

Ingredients

3 or 4 cloves of jumbo garlic

1 tbsp Maldon sea salt

20 strands of saffron

Splash of sherry vinegar

¼ lemon, juiced

3 egg yolks

325ml rapeseed or sunflower oil

Method

For best results use a kitchen blender. Aioli can be made by hand though; simply place a damp tea towel under the mixing bowl to stop it spinning while you whisk, as you'll need your other hand to pour the oil.

Add the garlic and salt to a blender and blitz to a paste (crush with a knife if not using a machine). Leave for ten minutes; this is important as it takes away some of the harshness of raw garlic.

In the meantime, pour a splash of boiling water over the saffron and let it infuse.

Then add the sherry vinegar, lemon juice and egg yolks to the blender and blitz for 30 seconds. Keeping the machine running, now add the oil in a slow steady stream until it's all incorporated. It should look like a mayonnaise.

Now add the saffron and water and pulse for a few seconds until incorporated. If the aioli is a little thick it's over mixed; the simple correction for this is just to add warm water until the desired consistency is achieved.

It can be stored in a sterilised screw top jar for up to 5 days in a fridge.

L'al Churrasco
PORTUGUESE BLACK PUDDING (MORCELA) AND ROAST PINEAPPLE PURÉE

Do not be frightened at the thought of making your own black pudding; it's a lot less daunting than you think, and the results are impressive! Any decent butchers will sell you the dried (pasteurised) blood mix you will need, but be sure to ask about salt levels already in the mix as they will vary.

Preparation time: 10 minutes | Cooking time: approx. 60-80 minutes | Serves: 8

Ingredients

For the black pudding:

250g dehydrated blood mix

70g vegetable suet

2 grated apples (choose a sharp/acidic variety)

1 tsp ground white pepper

1 tsp ground all-spice

1 tsp salt (if using a low seasoned blood mix; omit if already well salted)

½ tsp ground cinnamon

½ tsp ground ginger

600ml cold water

30g pine nuts

A few sprigs of fresh thyme

For the purée:

Half a fresh pineapple

Salt and pepper

Drizzle of extra-virgin olive oil

Knob of butter

Method

Combine all the ingredients for the black pudding, and press the mix into a deep-sided dish or tray (which has been lined with baking paper if not non-stick) so it's in a 4-6cm layer.

For best results, place the filled dish in a larger tray and pour warm water into the larger tray to a depth of 5cm. This effectively creates a bain-marie and ensures the pudding does not overcook.

Bake at 140°c (or at 110°c if not using the bain-marie method) for approximately 60-80 minutes. To check the pudding is cooked, poke a thermometer into the centre; it should read 85°c. If you don't have a meat thermometer, poke a thin knife into the centre instead and see if it comes out clean, as you would with a cake. The surface of the pudding should be firm to the touch.

As the black pudding cooks, prepare the roast pineapple purée.

Top and tail the pineapple, and trim off the skin and tough outer edge. Cut the pineapple into eighths along the length, removing the core if it's too firm. Season the pieces with salt and freshly ground pepper, drizzle with extra-virgin olive oil, and place in a roasting tray with a knob of butter.

Cover with a tightly fitting lid or tin foil and roast at 140°c for approximately 1 hour. Remove the foil or lid and continue to roast the pineapple until it turns a deep orange colour. Place the pineapple in a blender and blend for ten minutes, adding a little water as needed to adjust the consistency, until you have a thick purée.

The black pudding is ready to eat when cooked, however, frying 1cm slices in a little oil will give added texture and flavour to the completed dish.

Serve with the roast pineapple purée for a wonderful, homemade Portuguese treat!

Garden of DELIGHTS

From humble beginnings as a tea room in the Hazel Dene Garden Centre, Mrs Miller's Culgaith has steadily improved and developed over the years to become a restaurant renowned for excellence and its daily changing menus, based on fantastic local produce and a very committed chef...

When James Cowin and his brother Edward were growing up, Hazel Dene Garden Centre, not unlike most others in Cumbria at the time, was a lovely place to pick up your bedding plants on a Saturday afternoon, but not one you could stop at for lunch. James and Edward's entrepreneurial dad decided in the 1990s that an expansion was in order, and created a tea room which they named after its first cook – Mrs Miller, who just so happened to be the boys' school dinner lady! Cakes and teas, sandwiches and soups comprised the wholesome menu, and it was here that while roped into helping out with the washing up on weekends, young James decided that he would quite like to become a chef.

Having trained at Carlisle College for three years, the last of which saw him awarded Student of the Year, James went on to work at a Michelin-starred restaurant in Cumbria for two years. He has now been head chef at Mrs Miller's for nearly 15 years and takes great pride in continuing the success of the family business, along with his wife Rebecca front-of-house, and Edward who now runs the garden centre since their dad's well-deserved retirement. Eight years ago, James oversaw a revamp of the restaurant, which is now comprised of a 'living room' and 'conservatory' – cosy, homely and light, airy spaces respectively for dining at any time of the day. Rather aptly, the building which houses the restaurant has a long history of food production, having been a dairy, a cheese-maker's and then a game processing plant which sent its plucked products down the Settle-Carlisle railway line that runs alongside the building.

Today, Mrs Miller's enjoys a good rapport with similar local suppliers – James will generally ring round the local butchers and farms, and the fishmonger at Penrith, each morning and then create his daily menu around what's particularly good that day. In the summer this can even mean using up a glut of fruit and vegetables from the garden centre itself! The head chef likes to incorporate modern techniques into traditional dishes, and ensures that the food retains 'a touch of familiarity' so that customers from near and far feel at home. The restaurant is flexible enough to accommodate early birds for proper cooked breakfasts, those popping by for a snack or light lunch, and evening bookings on Fridays and Saturdays.

Named North-West Local Restaurant of the Year by the Waitrose Good Food Guide in 2017, Mrs Miller's appearance and setting may deceive some first-time visitors – many of whom travel for miles to dine there, with its growing reputation spreading far and wide – but this true gem, has been kept in the family and preserved all that is best about its humble origins through the years. Most importantly of all, it still serves very good food!

Mrs Miller's Tea Room

Freshly Baked Scones
* Scone Deal *
* Fruit or Cheese Scone *
served with butter and preserve
with Tea or Small Americano

Butterfactory
Artists
www.butterfactory.co.uk

More Big Forks

Mrs Miller's Culgaith
ROAST RUMP OF HERB-CRUSTED LAKE DISTRICT LAMB

This dish makes great use of the fantastic lamb that we have available to us here in the Eden valley. The lamb we use at Mrs Miller's comes from just down the road. Served with creamed flageolet beans and winter vegetables, and accentuated by the meat juices mingled with fresh garden mint, this is a gorgeous dish celebrating some wonderful seasonal flavours.

Preparation time: 30 minutes | Cooking time: approx. 1 hour | Serves: 4

Ingredients

4 lamb rumps

Salt and pepper

3 sprigs of rosemary

5 cloves of garlic

100ml olive oil

200g breadcrumbs

A handful of soft green herbs (sage, parsley, dill, chives, tarragon or basil for example)

1 sprig of thyme

1 small onion, cut into small dice

1 carrot, cut into small dice

Vegetable oil

1 courgette, cut into small dice

1 x 400g tin of flageolet beans, drained

50ml cream

500ml thickened lamb stock

1 tsp redcurrant jelly

A handful of fresh mint

1 tbsp Cumberland honey mustard

Method

Start by trimming most of the fat from the lamb rumps, but not all. Place into a plastic tub or a non-metallic roasting dish and season with salt and pepper, two sprigs of rosemary (coarsely chopped) and two cloves of garlic (smashed with a knife). Pour over the olive oil and mix well with your hands to ensure all the flavours get to know each other. Place to one side to allow the lamb to come to room temperature.

Place one peeled and chopped garlic clove, the breadcrumbs and the soft green herbs into a food blender. Pick the remaining rosemary and thyme leaves off the stalk and add to the blender. Pulse until you have a nice bright green herb crumb. Place into a bowl and keep to one side.

Place the diced onion and carrot into a pan with a splash of vegetable oil, a pinch of salt and one clove of garlic (crushed with the back of a knife). Sweat over a low heat until the carrots are soft, then add the courgettes and cook until all the vegetables are tender. Set aside.

Preheat the oven to 200°c and heat an ovenproof pan on the hob. Remove any excess herbs and garlic from the lamb, place the pieces into the pan fat side down and start to colour. The fat should start to turn nice and golden and render down. Once the fat is golden, place the lamb into the preheated oven for 14 minutes. Then remove the pan from the oven and leave in a warm place to rest and finish cooking through. The resting of the meat is very important for both texture and flavour.

While the lamb is resting, rinse the beans well, then place them into the pan the lamb was cooked in, having discarded any excess fat. Add the precooked vegetables, cream, thickened lamb stock and redcurrant jelly and bring to the boil. When you have a sauce-like consistency, sieve and add the mint. Keep the sauce warm while finishing the lamb rumps. Place them into the roasting tray fat side down and cover the top with a thin layer of the mustard and a nice coating of herb crust. Place back in the oven for 5 minutes.

To serve

Place the beans, vegetables and cream onto a high heat and cook until the cream starts to reduce and coat the vegetables, and ensure the sauce is hot. Remove the lamb from the oven and divide each piece into 3 or 4 slices. Rest whilst you divide the creamed beans and vegetables between four plates then place the lamb on top. Finish with the sauce.

Culinary CURATORS

The Old Stamp House is an Ambleside restaurant inspired by the food culture and heritage of Cumbria, and is run to much regional and nationwide acclaim by a team who are passionate about serving the food they know and love.

For Ryan and Craig Blackburn, hospitality runs in the family as much as the Lakes heritage they grew up surrounded by in the Great Langdale valley. Their grandparents ran hotels, and their parents presided over a local historic pub before setting up Stockghyll Fine Foods, a deli in Ambleside which you can find out more about in this book! So Ryan was following a well-trodden path when he studied business and then trained as a chef 'on the job' at establishments across the county, before teaming up with Craig to realise their ambition of running their own restaurant.

They set up The Old Stamp House in 2014 in a venue with some very Cumbrian history of its own; the unassuming building is the former workplace of none other than William Wordsworth, in his slightly less poetic role as distributor of stamps for Westmorland. Partly due to its listed status, and partly due to Ryan's passion for showcasing Lake District heritage, renovations were minimal in the intimate below-ground space the restaurant occupies, and a rustic feel remains along with the original flagstone flooring and Cumbrian artwork on the walls.

The premise behind The Old Stamp House is food inspired by Cumbria; most of the team are locals and their knowledge and passion have seen the restaurant win regional awards as well as gain nationwide recognition in the short time it has been open. As much of the produce as possible is sourced from within the county, including Herdwick hogget from Yew Tree Farm and game from John Stott at Cartmel Valley. They also use the small fishing fleets at Barrow and Whitehaven for fresh, local seafood and shellfish, and even collect ingredients such as wild herbs and mushrooms from the surrounding woodlands and fells.

For chef patron Ryan, curating these strong relationships with the suppliers and producers in his home county is where he finds real enjoyment. The compact seasonal menus change regularly – except for the Herdwick and shrimp dishes, which are absolute favourites of both staff and customers – based on the produce available. Everyone at The Old Stamp House is focused towards giving people a dining experience that truly reflects the food culture and landscape of Cumbria in all its diversity, bringing the traditional up to date with "as little manipulation as possible" as Ryan puts it, and finding more ways to celebrate the wonderful heritage that surrounds them.

Old Stamp House Restaurant
Food Inspired By Cumbria

The Old Stamp House

POTTED SHRIMP, CAULIFLOWER AND SPICED MEAD VELOUTÉ

This dish has been on the menu since Ryan and Craig started The Old Stamp House, and remains there as both the customers and staff love the dish. The recipe was created to use the brown shrimps – a famous local delicacy found in Morecambe Bay – and Ryan devised a sauce using mead, which works so well with the shrimps.

Preparation time: 20 minutes | Cooking time: approx. 1 hour | Serves: 6

Ingredients

For the cauliflower purée:

1 large cauliflower

100g butter

100ml double cream

For the velouté:

50g butter

1 banana shallot

1 tbsp mild madras curry powder

375ml honey mead (we use Harvest Gold)

400ml chicken stock

400ml fish stock

400ml double cream

For the potted shrimps:

1 lemon

100g butter

Pinch of mace

Pinch of cayenne pepper

1 tsp paprika

100g brown shrimps, peeled and cooked (preferably from Morecambe Bay)

For the garnish:

25g salted almonds

25g golden raisins, soaked in 50ml of mead

Method

For the cauliflower purée

Finely slice the cauliflower. In a large pan, melt the butter and add the shredded cauliflower with a pinch of salt. Gently cook, then when tender add the cream and reduce by half. Transfer the cauliflower to a blender and blend until you have a smooth purée. Adjust the seasoning and pass through a sieve. Keep warm until needed.

For the velouté

Melt the butter in the pan until it starts to foam, then slice the shallot and add to the pan. Cook gently until the shallot has softened. Add the mild madras curry powder and cook out, stirring continually, for 30 seconds. Add the mead to the pan and reduce by half. Once reduced, add the two stocks and reduce by half again. Once reduced, add a pinch of salt and the double cream. Bring to the boil and then pass through a fine sieve.

For the potted shrimps

Cut the lemon in half and place into a pan cut side down. Dice the butter and add to the pan along with the spices (the quantities can be adjusted to suit your personal preference). Place the pan on the heat and cook until the butter has melted and coloured and the lemon is caramelised, then set aside to cool. Place the shrimps in a large bowl then pour in the cooled butter and squeeze in the lemon juice. Mix with a spoon until the shrimps are evenly coated.

To serve

Pipe or spoon some purée into the bottom of the bowl, place some shrimp on top, add some raisins and almonds to the bowl and pour in the warmed sauce.

Come and POP IN

Poppi Red is a café and gift shop welcoming visitors to Hawkshead with a fun, bubbly atmosphere and freshly made cakes for everyone to enjoy.

Poppi Red was inspired by owner Kim's travels around the world, and her love of finding unique cards and gifts in places that you could browse in for hours. After returning home and daydreaming about how to recreate her experiences, Kim converted an art gallery in the lively village of Hawkshead into her own shop – a treasure trove of unusual things and pretty presents – which has since gone from strength to strength.

Customers are drawn in by the fantastic colour – courtesy of Kim's favourite flower and her own red hair! – as well as aromas of freshly ground coffee and home baked treats. The gift emporium is full of pottery, jewellery, scarves, knitwear, cushions, books, cards and much more; perfect for exploring and treating yourself as well as friends and loved ones. And speaking of treating yourself, the friendly and welcoming tea room is handily situated within the shop for a light bite or tasty lunch.

Everything is made to order from the food menu, and Poppi Red uses as much local produce as possible; the café is especially well known for its sausage rolls, made daily with Cumberland meat, and the scones that pair beautifully with jams and chutneys sourced from the village itself. Bread is delivered from a nearby artisan bakery, and the range of homemade cakes includes plenty of gluten-free and dairy-free options. The café is even licensed, serving local beers as well as a renowned 'Gin Sling' and Damson Fizz made with a Cumbrian tipple.

Hawkshead is a popular walker's destination, with something to suit everyone. Biking, fishing, riding and the Beatrix Potter connection sees Poppi Red busy all year round with tourists, regular customers and four legged visitors alike. The café and shop are dog friendly and even have treats available, as long as muddy paws stay on the floor! In warmer weather, the terrace outside is a wonderful place to relax and enjoy the views, so you can be certain of a great welcome whatever the season at the unique café and shop.

Poppi Red

Poppi Red
GLUTEN-FREE & DAIRY-FREE CHOCOLATE AND ORANGE CAKE

Chocolate and orange are a perfect match, and substituting the dairy products and normal flour with dairy- and gluten-free alternatives means no one misses out on this delicious sponge cake.

Preparation time: 15 minutes | Cooking time: 1½ hours | Serves: 8

Ingredients

For the sponge:

1 large orange

200g ground almonds

250g caster sugar

50g cocoa powder

½ tsp baking soda

½ tsp baking powder

6 eggs

For the dairy-free topping:

450g dairy-free spread (we use Vitalite)

1 orange, zested

Icing sugar

Method

Place the whole orange in a saucepan, cover with water, and boil for about 30 minutes or until soft. Blitz the orange in a food processor and combine this thoroughly with the rest of the sponge ingredients. Pour the cake mixture into a round 20cm cake tin, and bake in a preheated oven for approximately 45 minutes at 170°c. Cool for 10 minutes or so in the tin, then cool completely on a wire rack.

To make the icing, beat the spread with enough icing sugar to make the mixture smooth and glossy. Stir in the orange zest until well distributed.

When the cake is cooled, top the sponge with a generous amount of the orange icing, serve and enjoy.

From passion
TO PORTERAGE

The Porterage Co. is an independent wine merchant with shops in two locations, supplying Cumbria with friendly, knowledgeable and enjoyable shopping experiences for any occasion that calls for wine, gin, craft ale and lovely local accompaniments.

The Porterage Co. was founded by Colin Cropley, with his wife and business partner Judy, as an independent wine merchant, which now has two personality-filled shops and a trusted wholesale operation spanning Cumbria. Their ethos is to offer a shopping experience – whatever the occasion – that makes choosing and buying wines an enjoyable and leisurely activity, helped along by passionate and informed people who are keen to pass along their expertise. Colin developed a passion for the world of wine as a student visiting Italy, but chose the Lake District for its combination of beautiful scenery and unique culinary leanings as the perfect spot to open up his own business.

The flagship shop in Greenodd, equidistant from both Lake Windermere and Coniston Water, was fully renovated before opening in 2010 to create a welcoming atmosphere and eclectic space complete with a very friendly mascot, Meg the spaniel! Six years later, The Porterage Co. opened a second shop in Bowness-on-Windermere and continued to build its reputation for excellent service. "When we have listened to a customer and recommended a wine or beer, or matched to a food they are going to eat, they usually like them. We do try to cover all bases but cover them well; not just to have a wine from Greece, for example, but to have a wine we are really happy to sell from Greece. Over the years we have broadened customers' choices into many different areas of the world. I love to take people on a tasting journey" says Colin.

Both shops have a rustic feel with lots of wood, blackboards and a plethora of information for people to read; it's not unusual for a customer to lose themselves just in reading all the wine labels! The broad product range includes stacks of the bestsellers, bin-end bottles, magnums, single serves and even the odd jeroboam. In the evenings, the shops become venues for tasting masterclasses, but even daytime visits can be complemented by tasters from the range of over 40 gins, the selection of Cumbrian craft ales, or the wine and cheese offerings, of course.

Being an independent wine merchant means the team can work with small-production vineyards as well as bigger importers and have access to some fantastic, innovative suppliers, offering both excellent classic wines and contemporary portfolios for wholesale customers. Given the climate, no wine is made in Cumbria, so The Porterage Co. also champions craft ale, gins, vodkas, chutney, puddings, fudges, and anything else that is made in the Lake District and of great quality. "We support local wherever possible, as our business success is built on local people supporting us".

The Porterage Co.

Perfect pairings and THEIR STORY

Create the amazing recipes in this book and match with a flight of carefully selected wines, chosen by the knowledgeable wine experts from The Porterage Co., for a wonderful Cumbrian gastronomic experience!

PORTO RESTAURANT
Balsamic Cumbrian Chicken Livers
NERO D'AVOLA - Miopasso Nero D'Avola or Planeta Rossa, Italy

We suggest that a great grape match for these chicken liver beauties is Nero D'Avola - Sicily's red wine grape, with a ripe, spicy blackberry and damson character, soft tannins and just enough acidity. And if you're looking for something from one of the finest producers in Sicily and the best vintage in the last ten years, then Planeta Rosso is a fantastic choice. Alternatively, the deep purple-red Miopasso with its incredibly intense nose featuring black pepper and spices also offers a lovely match for liver, as it has an excellent balance, complexity and a soft, long finish.

STOCKGHYLL FINE FOODS
Ravenglass Crab and Marsh Samphire Quiche
ALBARINO - Lagar Do Frade Albarino, Spain

We at The Porterage Co. are big Albarino fans and believe this is one of Spain's most characterful white wines. A speciality of Rias Baixas in Galicia, you will find fascinating flavours of apricot, peach and grapefruit with a mineral note that adds vivacity, refreshing acidity on the palate and a lengthy finish. These wines are the perfect match for seafood dishes and may leave a pleasant lingering note of lemon zest. Lagar Do Frade is a beautiful glass of light yellow wine that is beautifully matched to the delicate crab and samphire flavours.

DODGSON WOOD
Maria's Mutton Koftas
SANGIOVESE - Bocelli Sangiovese IGT or Rubicone IGT Moma, Italy

Italian reds are fantastic food wines and Sangiovese is no exception. These wines exhibit a sweet and sour character and are an ideal partner for red meats in a tomato sauce, from meatballs to traditional ragu or Bolognese. Expect dense red fruits with Morello cherry and a whiff of herbs. The Bocelli family not only produce world-renowned opera singers but excellent wines as well, and this one is made by Andre Bocelli's brother! Our other recommendation is Rubicone IGT Moma (Sangiovese/Cabernet) blend; the cabernet adds flesh and might to Sangiovese's structure. Made by Umberto Cesari, one of Emillia Romagna's most awarded growers.

HIGGINSONS OF GRANGE
Higginson's Cumberland Coil with Grainy Mustard Mash and Root Vegetables
SHIRAZ (SYRAH) - Madfish Shiraz, Margaret River, Western Australia (5 stars at the Australian International Wine Show)

Shiraz has the clout to stand up to heavily seasoned meat and herbs; for example, Cumbria's very own Cumberland sausage, packed with pepper and aromatic rosemary. This MadFish Shiraz is full of dark cherry fruits with spicy peppery hints and an almost chocolatey character. The oak is restrained, and the palate is rich and concentrated without being heavy and tannic. A premium modern cool climate wine where both the juice and the packaging are right on the money.

MRS MILLER'S CULGAITH

Roast Rump of Herb-Crusted Lake District Lamb
TEMPRANILLO - Ramon Bilbao Rioja Crianza or Hugonel Rioja Reserva, Spain

A Tempranillo that has begun to mature so that it smells like autumn leaves goes with slow-cooked lamb like no other wine. In Rioja, 'Crianza' and 'Reserva' wines spend at least one year in oak barrels. This produces elegant barrel-aged reds, combining oak flavours with notes of wild strawberry and prune, and a mellow smoothness that will have a great affinity with the roast lamb and herbs. One of the best Crianzas on the market today is the Ramon Bilbao Rioja. Equally, the Hugonel Rioja Reserva is a real crowd pleaser for any occasion and superb value for money.

THE BOATHOUSE

Hake, Minted Peas and Chorizo Butter
CHARDONNAY - Domaine Paquet Macon Fuisse, Burgundy, France

The voluptuous curves of a Chardonnay would compliment the delicate flaky white fish flavours and richness and creaminess of the chorizo butter in this delicious dish. This ripeness would be offset by the fresh green accompaniments. The wines from the Maconnais area in Burgundy offer extremely good value in Burgundian terms. The Domaine Paquet Macon Fuisse has an amazing honeyed aroma with ripe pears and caramelised pineapple, as well as creamy nuances and a good mineral backbone. It is a Pouilly Fuisse 'lookalike' and is drinking beautifully now.

VIRGINIA HOUSE

Smoked Duck Breast with Damsons and Pistachio Dukkha
PINOT NOIR - Te Kairanga Pinot Noir (5 stars at New Zealand International Wine Show)

Just think of the fatty, melting flesh of duck cut through with a slightly chilled Pinot Noir - sensational! Pinot Noirs display amazing aromas of raspberry, cherry, strawberry and currants - the ultimate wine for duck. Dukkah is an Egyptian seasoning that has found its way out of the souks of Cairo and into kitchens all over the world. In the words of Aubert de Villaine, proprietor of Domaine de la Romanee Conti, 'Pinot Noir does not exist. It's a ghost.' The very best Pinots are just that; sublimely effortless, treading so lightly you experience it as a fluent and graceful song of a wine. We recommend Te Kairanga Pinot Noir from Martinborough where the soil is rich and the food is plentiful.

APPLEBY CREAMERY

Chicken Parcels Stuffed with Smoked Brie
CINSAULT - Rare Vinyards Cinsault Rosé, Languedoc, France

Chicken can be an 'anything goes' territory and is down to personal wine choice. This dry Southern French Rosé drinks very well, with flavours of bloomy-rind cheeses such as Brie or Camembert. Though very pale to look at and delicate to taste, this wine has an unexpected tenacity and hold, making it a perfect match for this chicken dish. The wine, from Languedoc, is cool-fermented and bottled early to capture the fresh summer berry fruits with a noticeable kick of wild strawberry. A very classy and enjoyable glass of Rosé made from 100% Cinsault.

THE APPLE PIE CAFÉ AND BAKERY

Bramley Apple Pie
GLERA - Galanti Prosecco Extra Dry DOC, Veneto, Italy

Real prosecco should taste of juicy, ripe pear flesh and feel light, clean and sparkly on your tongue like a melting snowflake. This extra dry prosecco from Galanti in Veneto is made with 100% Glera grapes and is 'spumante' meaning sparkling (some are 'frizzante' or semi-sparkling). The fizz will cut through the mellow sweetness of the apple pie and the fats in the pastry to provide a beautiful mouthful of pear and apple flavours with a fresh light acidity. Prosecco DOC (controlled designation of origin) is produced in the nine provinces spanning the Veneto and Friuli Venezia Giulia regions.

FIRST FLOOR CAFE

Fish Chowder
CHARDONNAY - Charles and Charles, Columbia Valley, Oregon, USA

A Chardonnay is a lovely match with mild, creamy chowder. Sometimes you only need a spoonful of cream in a dish to make Chardonnay the perfect choice. The Charles & Charles Chardonnay is a firm, juicy, refreshing wine that picks up great power and depth in your glass. There are aromas of Pippin apples, jasmine and some citrus along with warm caramel. These flavours intensify on the palate where they are joined by light tropical notes and a streak of minerality. Power meets finesse here. Charles and Charles was founded in 2008, and is a collaboration between Food & Wine Magazine's 2014 Winemaker of the Year, Charles Smith (Charles Smith Wines), and Charles Bieler (Three Thieves, Gotham Project).

CARTMEL CHEESES

Mrs Kirkham's Lancashire Cheese and Onion Pie
FALANGHINA - *Feudi di San Gregorio Albente Falanghina, Campania, Italy*

The Falanghina flavours meld gently with the sweet cooked onions in this dish and the wine has an ample texture that sits comfortably with the cheese. This wine is made with 100% Falanghina grape and so the palate is rich and fruity with a rounded texture and crisp, balancing acidity. It has a very clean finish; a beautiful sensation coupled with the cheese and pastry. One of the main protagonists in the renaissance of southern Italian wines, Feudi di San Gregorio has carved out a reputation for making truly world-class wines with flair, class and elegance.

HAWKSHEAD RELISH

Red Chicken Curry
RIESLING - *Juffer Riesling Kabinett, Paulinshof, Mosel, Germany*

With lime-scented curries, the lemony notes in a Riesling play off the citrus in the food, and the off-dry sweetness counteracts the warmth of the spices. This excellent Mosel wine shows an amazingly complex balance of fresh acidity and off-dry sweetness, slate-driven mineral texture, fresh fruit and a deep oily complexity. It has tremendous poise and depth and simply must be tried! Paulinshof, on the banks of the river Mosel, is a small producer of top quality, traditional style Rieslings. Owners Christa and Oliver Jungling work nine hectares of steep vineyard to produce sublime and delicate world class wines.

DODDS RESTAURANT

Saffron Seafood Risotto
PECORINO - *Terre di Chieti, Umani Ronchi, Abruzzo, Italy*

The pear and grapefruit flavours of the Pecorino with its strong aromatic notes and wonderful acidity are a perfect foil for this risotto with its subtle seafood component. Pecorino is a recently re-discovered grape variety, with a low yielding grape, and therefore exhibits great depth of flavour. Umani Ronchi has doubled its estate since the seventies, always setting itself ambitious wine quality objectives, and has been a stalwart of the Abruzzo region.

THE OLD STAMP HOUSE

Potted Shrimp, Cauliflower and Spiced Mead Veloute
CHARDONNAY - *Les Mougeottes, Vielles Vignes, Pays d'oc*

Chardonnay, with its buttery flavours and vanilla overtones, melds beautifully with the richness and strong flavour of potted shrimps and compliments the sweeter mead veloute. This Chardonnay is juicy and full flavoured. Les Mougeottes is one of the best impressions of a white Burgundy we have ever tasted (at a fraction of the price). Dry and rounded on the palate, with texture, richness and finesse, this wine has utter charm and completeness.

ROTHAY MANOR HOTEL & FINE DINING

Hogget Loin with Artichoke and Caramelised Onion
MALBEC - *Clos Troteligotte K-Or (Organic), Cahors, South West France*

An absolute stunner of a Malbec (from its original birthplace in Cahors) which has been lauded in Decanter, Wine Spectator and elsewhere! The powerful black plum and berry fruits tinged with a herbaceous complexity and a long firm finish would compliment the slowly cooked hogget beautifully, with enough rusticity to blend with the caramelised onions. This Malbec has a soft and rich mouthfeel with a lingering finish. Clos Troteligotte was certified organic in 2014 and is a modern style Cahors.

THE SQUARE ORANGE

Morbier Tartiflette
GRENACHE, SYRAH & CARIGNAN - *Côtes du Rhône Massif d'Uchaux, Rhone Valley, France*

The grape blend in this Côtes du Rhône, with ripe red-berried fruits set against a spicy backdrop, works beautifully with the rich mixture of cheese, cream and bacon in this wonderful Morbier Tartiflette. This is a cracking Côtes du Rhône that received a Silver Medal at a recent wine event in France. Massif d'Uchaux is one of the 'cult' wine making villages in the Côtes du Rhône.

DODDS RESTAURANT

Torta di Riso
MOSCATO - *Asti Spumante, Rifiessi, Piedmont, Italy*

This light dessert is crying out for an ice cold quality bottle of Asti Spumante. This sparkling wine is made from 100% Moscato Bianco grapes and is gently sweet and beautifully fruity which matches perfectly with this dessert. Torta di Riso, inspired by the British love of rice pudding, is one of Italy's favourite cold picnic food recipes, and a big part of Italian Easter time food customs. A simply mouth-watering combination of flavours!

L' AL CHURRASCO

Portuguese Black pudding (Morcela) and Roast Pineapple Purée
SYRAH / TRINCADEIRA - *Smart Dog, Alentejano, Portugal*

The minerality in this spicy, deep red wine is a perfect foil for the fattiness and salty components of this tasty, tangy black pudding dish. The fruitiness in the wine blends in nicely with the pineapple purée, creating a lovely mouthful of flavour. Juicy, clean and full of sweet fruit and spice, this enjoyable wine is dense and savoury on the palate with grainy tannins. Smart Dog is made by JP Ramos, a leading figure in the Alentejano region of Portugal.

A labour of
LOVE

After a full kitchen refurbishment and refreshed menu, Porto Restaurant has been busier than ever this year, serving its award-winning food to customers looking for a relaxed lunch spot, bistro or elegant à la carte evening menu in the beautiful village location.

Faye Ramsey opened Porto Restaurant seven years ago in the centre of Bowness-on-Windermere, and has run the business since then with an unremitting passion for food. Following her ten years of industry experience, during which she decided to return home to Cumbria from London, Porto opened its doors on Valentine's Day in 2011 after six months of building works. Always wanting to keep things fresh, relevant and interesting, recently Faye decided that it was once again time for a facelift, which meant refitting the restaurant kitchen and refocusing on what Porto is all about.

Lead by Faye and head chef Slav Miskiewicz, the team have used the refurbishment to start afresh, and have seen an increase in eager customers during the extended opening hours. The bistro style, à la carte and relaxed lunch menus feature the same fantastic food, best described as modern British with hints and influences from across the world's cuisines, but have been simplified by omitting unnecessary components to bring the focus back to the outstanding core flavours of each dish. The menus are very seasonal and always include specials, changing regularly according to the time of year, having been developed collaboratively by Faye and Slav.

Porto Restaurant makes the most of its idyllic location just five minutes from the Bowness shore of Lake Windermere, using the natural larder of the Cumbrian countryside to create dishes with produce such as cheeses, ice cream and damson liqueur which are all made locally. Even the salmon gravadlax, paired with blackberry syrup as one of the irresistible starters, is cured in Lakes Distillery gin! Faye herself brings in a fruitful harvest each year from the orchard in the grounds of her family home, including Victoria plums, rare pear varieties and berries.

As a Cumbrian born and bred, Faye enjoys being able to engage with the community through Porto Restaurant, linking with other businesses to run competitions and raise money for charities, as well as giving away prizes. Her ethos for the venture as a whole is one that values thoughtful decisions and a happy team, as the love and care they put in make for great service and wonderful food, and ensures that the dining experience at Porto Restaurant absolutely reflects this dedication to excellence.

Porto Restaurant

BALSAMIC CUMBRIAN CHICKEN LIVERS

Owner Faye and her head chef Slav were inspired to create this dish for Porto Restaurant by the natural larder in the Cumbrian countryside around them, full of wonderful natural ingredients. The balance of sweetness, sourness and acidity in the sauce is the perfect counterpart to the rich liver.

Preparation time: 15-20 minutes | Cooking time: 10 minutes | Serves: 4

Ingredients

400g free-range Cumbrian chicken livers

150g Cumbrian pancetta

100ml balsamic vinegar

25g clear honey

30ml cooking brandy

70g blackberries

20g fresh parsley, chopped

Salt and pepper, to taste

1 ciabatta roll

100g rocket leaves

Method

To prepare the ingredients, clean the chicken livers by removing any sinew or membrane, dice the pancetta into approximately 5mm cubes, and mix the balsamic, honey and brandy in a bowl.

Heat a little oil in a large pan on a medium to high heat and sear the livers with the pancetta until everything is golden brown but the livers are still rare. Add the blackberries and balsamic then reduce until thick and sticky. Add the chopped parsley, mix well and season to taste with salt and pepper.

Slice then toast the ciabatta and put it in the centre of the plate. Cover the bread with the liver and pancetta and garnish with rocket leaves. Enjoy!

It's all coming UP ROSES

Ambleside's two rosette, newly refurbished hotel with an emphasis on fine dining and treating yourself in style and comfort in the heart of the Lake District.

Rothay Manor has it all: luxury rooms; roaring fires; personable staff; dog-friendly spaces; and at the forefront of all this, fine dining that reflects the seasonality and locality of its Lakeland surroundings. The elegant country house has been a hotel for nearly six decades, but has had a new lease of life recently thanks to Jamie and Jenna Shail. The couple took on Rothay Manor with plenty of experience in the hospitality industry and a desire to bring the hotel, and especially its restaurant, right up to date.

With a long-term aim to establish Rothay Manor as a fine dining destination, renovations began in the kitchens and have been ongoing since Jamie and Jenna brought their vision to the timeworn building, the original parts of which date back to 1826. As their experienced general manager Peter notes, history usually "fights back" when you attempt to impose modernity on such a structure, so you have to expect the unexpected! Despite this, Rothay Manor can boast numerous individually decorated rooms and suites – all kitted out for the guest's absolute comfort, and some with beautiful balconies or private gardens – and a restaurant that exudes elegance and warmth.

More and more non-residents are coming to dine at the hotel, drawn by its growing reputation, either for the popular afternoon teas or exciting evening à la carte and tasting menus. Head chef Daniel and his kitchen team create new ideas using as much of the finest local produce as possible for inspiration. There are plenty of options for those fond of Herdwick lamb or fresh seafood, for example, as well as a dedicated menu for vegetarians.

Two AA rosettes and a team of staff who combine experience with energy, enthusiasm and fresh ideas are sure signs that Rothay Manor has embraced its new direction with a drive for excellence. To those who have moved forward with the hotel, what stands out, and hasn't changed over the years, is the uniquely friendly, welcoming and relaxed atmosphere. This encourages staff to interact with guests and get to know them, and feel comfortable. Whether you're dining in the restaurant or staying in the idyllic Ambleside location, Rothay Manor has set itself up with renewed vigour as the perfect place to retreat, to indulge, and most importantly, to enjoy yourself!

Rothay Manor

Rothay Manor
HOGGET LOIN WITH ARTICHOKE AND CARAMELISED ONION

Hogget refers to sheep between 1-2 years old, and is a delicious balance between tender lamb and full-flavoured mutton.

Preparation time: 4 hours | Cooking time: 3½ hours | Serves: 4

Ingredients

1 whole hogget shoulder

1kg onion

100g carrot, sliced

100g celery, sliced

100g leek, sliced

1 garlic bulb

1 sprig of thyme

750ml red wine

400g hogget loin, sinew and excess fat removed

Olive oil

100g onion, sliced

250g butter

4 baby globe artichoke

1 lemon

200ml chicken stock

600g Jerusalem artichoke

100g baby onions

10g sugar

Pinch of salt

200g spinach

Method

For the hogget shoulder
Place the shoulder into a deep ovenproof pan and add the onion, carrot, celery, leek, garlic, thyme and red wine and cover with a lid. Cook at 160°c for 3 hours or until falling off the bone. Pull the meat apart and dress with the hogget sauce when ready.

For the hogget loin
Roll the loin tightly in cling film and rest in the fridge for an hour, or until required. Slice into four portions of 100g each. Cook the loin in a hot pan with a little oil; colour the meat on all sides then baste in foaming butter until cooked to your preference.

For the onion purée
On a low heat, sweat the onions until translucent, add 50g of butter and 200ml of water and cover with a cartouche. Simmer for 1 hour, blend to a smooth purée and season.

For the globe artichoke
Remove the outer leaves and peel the stalk, leaving 3cm of it attached for presentation. Place the prepared artichoke in cold water with a squeeze of lemon juice. When ready, cook in seasoned chicken stock until tender; around 5 minutes at a gentle simmer.

For the pot roasted Jerusalem artichoke
Wash 400g of the artichokes and cut in half lengthways. Season and oil a heavy-based saucepan, and place the artichokes cut side down in it. Roast until coloured on a high heat, then add 50g of butter, cover to create steam, and cook the artichokes until tender. Remove from heat and set aside.

For the crispy artichoke skins
Bake 200g of the Jerusalem artichokes with a little water in the bottom of an oven tray at 170°c for 90 minutes. Scoop out the centres and reserve (they make a particularly good soup.) Dehydrate the skins in the oven at the lowest temperature available, ensuring they do not colour. Once dry, deep fry at 200°c until golden and crisp, and season to taste.

For the caramelised baby onion
Halve the onions, leaving the skin on. Sprinkle the sugar, salt, a drizzle of oil and 15g of diced butter into a frying pan. Place the onions cut side down in the pan, and slowly caramelise until golden in colour and cooked through; this should take around 5 minutes on a low heat. Remove from the pan, take off the skins and any root then set aside.

For the hogget sauce
Skim any remaining fat from the shoulder cooking liquor, and reduce (this should have a shine and become substantially thicker.)

To serve
Wilt the spinach in a hot pan and season to taste. Ensure that all the other components of the dish are hot and the loin has had time to rest. Place three dots of onion purée onto the plate, then add the pot roast artichoke and the baby onions nearby, following the flow of the plate. Place two pieces of the flaked shoulder in between and rest the sliced loin on top of this. Use the globe artichokes and spinach to weave between all the elements and bring the whole dish together. Finish with the crispy skins for texture and the glossy hogget sauce.

Small but perfectly FORMED

Shed 1 is a small batch gin distillers, working from an actual garden shed, which belongs to Andy and Zoe Arnold-Bennett. They create smooth, bold but balanced gins which are stocked across Cumbria in discerning shops and bars, restaurants and hotels.

Having both worked abroad as an actor and a teacher respectively, husband and wife Andy and Zoe were keen to embark on a new business that would enable them to stay at home. As Andy puts it, when you live in a place as beautiful as the Cumbrian countryside, you don't want to stay away for too long! So, after Zoe introduced Andy to a classic gin and tonic, as well as the delights of homemade damson and sloe gin, Andy began to experiment with compound gins – those you can make at home without a license.

The distillery came into being when the couple realised they could fit a gin still in one of the two sheds in their back garden. Shed 1 was closest to the house, hence the name, and from there Andy and Zoe now create thirty-six 50cl bottles of handcrafted gin per run in the seven square foot space. They don't do distillery tours though, as there's only just enough room for Andy, the sole gin maker, to do his work!

Shed 1's three standard gins were born out of experiences or events that inspired Andy and Zoe. Fancy Frolic harks back to summer walks with their dog on the beach and tastes of strawberry, ginger and lime. Giggle in the Ginnel, which Andy and Zoe dreamt up for a party in the alleyway alongside

their house, features star anise and elderberry. From angelica root to cardamom pods, Shed 1 uses a range of interesting botanicals from specialist suppliers, as well as water from the nearby Eden valley, to create gins which are smooth enough to sip, yet bold enough to mix. The flavours are beautifully balanced too, as evidenced by the third standard gin, Cuckold's Revenge, which won a two star Great Taste Award in 2017 for its layers of warming spice and citrus.

Experimentation, taste testing with a few lucky friends, and trial batches are the main stages a Shed 1 product goes through before it joins the official line up. For the future, Andy is looking to collaborate with a friend who recently opened a flower growing business to create a new seasonal gin. The existing specials are Festive Tipple – which is referred to as 'Christmas in a glass' by customers – and the aptly named Shed Loads of Love for Valentine's Day. With stockists across the whole of Cumbria and a few more besides, as well as a wholesale distributor, Shed 1 is successfully making its mark on the gin scene in Cumbria, despite being the smallest distiller there!

Shed 1
FESTIVE TIPPLE SORBET

This refreshing sorbet uses one of our seasonal special gins, and would work wonderfully as a palate-cleansing dessert after a festive feast.

Preparation time: 10 minutes, plus freezing time | Serves: 6

Ingredients

120ml water

100g sugar

620ml tonic water

120ml Shed 1 Festive Tipple Gin

Method

Put the water and sugar into a pan and heat until sugar has dissolved, then take off the heat and allow to cool. Add the tonic water and gin and give it a stir.

If you have an ice cream maker, follow the manufacturer's instructions on how to freeze. If you don't, pour the mixture into a tub, place in the freezer and mix the sorbet regularly with a fork as it freezes to break up the ice crystals.

Shed 1
GIGGLE BEER

Our lovely star anise and elderberry gin, used as the basis for a fabulous cocktail in this recipe, is available all year round. Whether you're celebrating in summery or wintery weather, this will really add some pizazz to your parties!

Preparation time: 5 minutes | Serves: 1

Ingredients

50ml Giggle in the Ginnel

10ml Sambuca

A dash of lime cordial

Root beer, to top up (we use Bundaberg)

Method

Put a few cubes of ice into a tall glass, add all the ingredients and give it a good stir. Garnish with a slice of lime. Cheers!

Continental & Cumbrian FUSION

Slate Bar & Café serves up a selection of classic cocktails, coffee and lunch platters along with generous helpings of continental hospitality in the historic town of Kendal.

You can find Slate, one of Kendal's newest café bars, nestled in the beautiful Wainwright's Yard, the custom designed outdoor area in the heart of the town that plays host to high-end shopping, and now to a unique place where both locals and visitors can enjoy a drink and a nibble with friends in casual yet sophisticated style. For private events, there's a whole mezzanine available to hire which makes for a pretty spectacular venue whether you're partying or talking business. The warm welcome and table service set Slate Bar and Café apart on any occasion, which was the aim of owners Kaushik and Tejshree Mistry. They have cherry-picked European café bar culture and married those influences with local artisan produce to create a daytime retreat or an evening out in Kendal to remember.

Slate offers a menu of classic cocktails made with premium products, a varied selection of more than 40 gins, 22 carefully chosen wines all available by the glass and freshly roasted coffee, sourced from the experts just down the road at Carvetii. The monthly gin tastings are hugely popular, so booking is a must if you're partial to a G&T. There's no need to look elsewhere for dinner either, as platters of charcuterie, local cheeses, vegetarian antipasti, and fresh bread from nearby bakery Staff of Life are sure to satisfy all tastes. And when they've whet your appetite, you won't want to miss the complimentary Friday evening buffets, which provide the perfect opportunity for a well-earned wind down with your after work drink. During the day there are soups, sandwiches and salads to sample for lunch, with handmade cakes to follow. In true continental fashion, the little treats that arrive with your drinks make doubly sure that no one goes hungry!

Kaushik and Tejshree love to travel across the globe, bringing back experiences of both the countries they've holidayed in and the UK cities they've lived in. The vibrant atmosphere of metropolitan bars and the hospitality of laid-back European cafés mingle perfectly at the stylish yet relaxed café bar, in large part due to the staff who work there. Slate is "really all about people" says Kaushik, who describes his team as "very geared towards having a good time and looking after the customers." The emphasis on personality has created an atmosphere people simply want to spend time enjoying, and makes Slate the perfect spot to eat, drink, chat and have a good time.

Slate Bar & Café
TOFFEE FLAT WHITE MARTINI

This indulgent cocktail is perfect for coffee-lovers, but the sweetness that comes through from the toffee vodka makes it irresistible to anyone!

Preparation time: 5 minutes | Serves: 1

Ingredients

35ml toffee vodka

25ml Baileys

Double shot of Carvetii coffee (cooled)

Method

Shake all the ingredients in a cocktail shaker with ice, making sure the coffee is cool before it's mixed with the Baileys.

Shake hard and then double strain into a martini glass.

Garnish with 3 coffee beans placed in a triangle.

CUCUMBER AND ELDERFLOWER COLLINS

In contrast to the martini, this gin cocktail is so refreshing, full of light flavours and perfect for summer evenings.

Preparation time: 5 minutes | Serves: 1

Ingredients

4 slices of cucumber

10ml sugar syrup

20ml lemon juice

35ml Slate Gin

50ml fresh apple juice

15ml St-Germain Elderflower Liqueur

Method

In a cocktail shaker, first muddle the cucumber and sugar syrup.

Then add all the other ingredients and 6 or 7 cubes of ice. Shake vigorously.

Pour into a tall glass and garnish with cucumber.

Bring me
SUNSHINE

The Square Orange serves up a slice of continental café culture – complete with a full bar, speciality coffee menu and live music evenings – along with fresh, authentic, Neapolitan-style pizza and other European delights in the heart of Keswick.

Established in 1998, many would say that The Square Orange was ahead of its time, bringing true continental style café bar culture into what was a very traditional Lakeland town. Although it's not actually square, it certainly is orange, and bursting with the joy, warmth and sense of fun that this colour is associated with on the continent. The lively atmosphere mingles with the friendly chatter of Lakeland locals and visitors from all over the world; the appeal of the "Squorange" (as it's affectionately known) lies in the fact that people can walk in not knowing a soul, yet feel immediately welcomed.

James Hutchinson owns The Square Orange, and was joined four years ago by experienced chef and general manager Karl Phillips, who keeps the business moving forwards and the ideas rolling in along with James' wife Jenni. The open kitchen behind the bar means all the cooking is on show, which makes the operation pretty slick but somewhat cosy at times. Despite strong competition for space, The Square Orange also boasts a corner pizza oven, where handmade dough is transformed into hugely popular stonebaked pizzas. A mix of Spanish tapas, Italian antipasti, Greek mezze and specials 'of the moment' completes the unique and eclectic food menu.

The café bar's international influences are reflected in the quality of the food and drink, partly due to some excellent Spanish and Italian suppliers, as well as local suppliers who import great produce from Europe. Local microbreweries sit alongside the Belgian and German beer on tap, as well as guest wines from family-run vineyards. The Square Orange supports great independent producers whether at home or abroad, such as rotating coffee blends from Cumbrian roasteries. And they can't mention coffee without highlighting the owner's healthy if not slightly obsessive interest in it; James also runs Lakes Coffee Services, which maintains and services coffee machinery and provides barista training for many coffee businesses in the county.

Whether you're after a quick coffee and some quiet time, an afternoon game of scrabble or an authentic Neopolitan pizza with friends and family, it is near impossible to leave without having enjoyed some friendly banter between neighbouring tables. Atmosphere is paramount at The Square Orange, as the team believe that a business like theirs is not just about great food and drink: the journey; the whole package; the heart and soul of the place are what make their café bar special.

The Square Orange
MORBIER TARTIFLETTE

We've put our own twist on this 'modern day classic' which originated in the French Alps. It's the ultimate comfort food after a chilly autumn or winter's day on our Cumbrian fells. The rich and indulgent combination of potato, cheese and pancetta makes this dish an ideal side or main.

Preparation time: 15 minutes | Cooking time: 45 minutes | Serves: 8 as a side or 4 as a main

Ingredients

1.2kg waxy potatoes, skin on and thinly sliced

2 garlic cloves (1 whole, 1 crushed)

2 sprigs of thyme

2 tbsp butter

1 onion, thinly sliced

300g smoked pancetta (or smoked bacon) lardons

150ml dry white wine

500ml double cream

400g Morbier cheese, diced (or similar semi-soft tangy French cheese)

Salt and pepper, to season

Chives, to garnish

Method

Preheat the oven to 200°c. Place the potatoes, whole garlic clove and 1 sprig of thyme in a pan of boiling salted water for about 10 minutes or until parboiled. Set aside to drain in a colander (remove the thyme and garlic).

Meanwhile, heat the butter in a large saucepan and add the onion. Allow to sweat for about 8 minutes, then add the smoked pancetta lardons, crushed garlic and remaining thyme and cook till browned. Add the wine to this pan to deglaze it, and then add 500ml of cream, the parboiled potatoes and 300g of the diced Morbier.

Gently simmer for about 20 minutes, stirring occasionally, until the wine, cream and cheese have blended into a beautiful sauce but the potato slices still hold their shape. Season to taste.

Carefully spoon the mixture into individual dishes or one medium-sized gratin dish, layering the potato, onion and sauce. Sprinkle the remaining 100g of Morbier on top of mixture and bake the tartiflette in the oven for about 8 minutes. Garnish with a sprinkle of chopped chives.

To serve

Serve with warm crusty bread, salad, cooked meats and pickles and enjoy with a glass of Savoie wine or even a cheeky Belgian beer!

Family FINERY

Stockghyll Fine Food is a deli with a difference; fresh food made daily and specialist ingredients sourced locally by a husband and wife team who love to celebrate the best of Cumbrian cuisine as well as artisanal produce from around the UK and Europe.

Margaret and Philip Blackburn had accumulated a wealth of experience working in the hospitality industry by the time they decided to follow their own dream and set up a little family-run deli in Ambleside. The husband and wife team opened Stockghyll Fine Food in 2015, and have since built up a strong local following in the heart of the Lake District. Along with daughter Olivia, their reputation as purveyors of great produce offering great service has only grown; some customers pop in every day to sample their favourites from the fresh deli counter, or pick up some of the more specialist ingredients that find their way onto the shelves from all over Cumbria and beyond.

Margaret has a particular knack for sourcing these unusual, high-quality products, having formed a network of local suppliers to ensure she can always find the very best food and drink around. Some of these suppliers also work with The Old Stamp House, the restaurant in Ambleside run by Ryan and Craig Blackburn, who are Margaret and Phillip's sons, proving that good taste does run in the family! Margaret also makes her own gingerbread vodka, which Ryan uses in some of the delicious desserts on the restaurant menu. The fruitful relationship works both ways, as cuts of meat that don't get used in The Old Stamp House's kitchen are readily made into pasties at the deli, such as the Herdwick lamb creation that's "a real taste of the fells".

It may not be surprising to hear, with all the mentions of such culinary delights, that Phil is also a chef, and creates freshly baked goods himself every morning for the deli to sell. The hugely popular pies and pasties, quiches, sausage rolls, Scotch eggs, artisan breads and other delicacies soon disappear as customers spy them in the window display, or laid out in the fresh counter. The family's love for quality local produce shines through in all aspects of Margaret and Phil's thriving business.

With pick-and-mix style antipasti, regional cheeses, hand-selected local ales and spirits (many from nearby microbreweries) and a wide selection of groceries, including gluten-free options, the deli is a veritable Aladdin's Cave for foodies and keen cooks. Cumbria is well-represented, and so is the rest of UK, along with Spain, France and Italy. Whether you're a lucky Ambleside native or from a little further afield, fine food in the Lake District doesn't get much more tempting than this.

Stockghyll Fine Food

Stockghyll Fine Food
RAVENGLASS CRAB AND MARSH SAMPHIRE QUICHE

This quiche was developed so that we could use local crab meat from Ravenglass, combined with wild foraged samphire found on the marshes in June, July and August. Here in Cumbria we are lucky to have many fine artisan suppliers and we use local butter and Lakeland free range eggs in this recipe. Out of season, marsh samphire is available from a good quality greengrocer.

Preparation time: 30 minutes, plus 30 minutes chilling time | Cooking time: 20 minutes | Makes: 1 x 25cm quiche or 2 x 10cm quiches

Ingredients

For the shortcrust pastry:

300g plain flour

150g Cumbrian unsalted butter

Pinch of salt

Cold water

For the filling:

100g Ravenglass white crab meat

5 stems of fresh foraged marsh samphire

4 Cumbrian free-range eggs

100ml full-fat milk or cream

100g Thornby Moor Cumbrian farmhouse cheese, grated

Salt and ground black pepper

Method

For the pastry

Preheat the oven to 150°c. To make the pastry, sift the flour and a good pinch of salt into a bowl, then rub in the butter with your fingertips until the mixture resembles fine breadcrumbs. Gradually add 125ml of cold water, continuously mixing until it comes together to form a rough dough, adding a splash more water if needed. Bring it together with your hands, wrap in cling film and place in the fridge for 30 minutes.

Use a non-stick tart tin or lightly grease the base and sides of a normal tart tin. Line the tin with pastry, pushing down lightly on the bottom and into the sides. Lightly prick the base of the tart with a fork, line the tart case with a large circle of greaseproof paper or foil, and fill with baking beans. Blind bake the tart for 20 minutes, remove the paper and beans, repair any cracks with leftover pastry, then continue to cook for 5-10 minutes until golden brown.

For the filling

Rinse the samphire well under running water, remove the woody ends and cut the remainder into lengths of 2-3cm. Layer the crab meat over the pastry base, then add the samphire. You can increase the quantity of crab meat to your own taste, but ensure that the samphire is covered with the egg mixture to prevent burning. Beat the eggs well with the cream or milk and season with salt and black pepper. Add the grated cheese then pour the mixture into the case over the crab meat and samphire. Bake in the oven for 20 minutes. Leave to cool slightly and serve warm, or refrigerate and serve cold.

Expect the UNEXPECTED

Comprising a fine dining restaurant, gin parlour, and rooms, Virginia House epitomises relaxed elegance and invites guests to enjoy a uniquely personalised gastronomic experience.

Whether it's a time for eating, for drinking, or for resting, Virginia House is the perfect place to find joy in all three, thanks to the beautifully crafted world its proprietors have created. Craig and Louise Sherrington welcome diners, visitors and gin-lovers alike to share their passion for wonderful food, great service and a sense of occasion at the fine dining restaurant, gin parlour and rooms. The couple bought Virginia House in 2015, having instantly fallen in love with the 18th century building when searching for an opportunity to make their own mark on the Cumbrian gastronomic scene.

In the restaurant, you can find locally foraged ingredients and fresh market produce sharing the limelight on the dynamic tasting menus that are inspired by seasonality as much as by the natural larder of Cumbria. The food at Virginia House is meant for more than just consuming; it can be evocative and thought-provoking, taking people on a unique culinary journey and appealing to all the senses. The intimate dining space of just 34 covers is looked after by Louise, who is front of house, though Craig often takes time out of the kitchen to chat with guests about the dishes.

Michelin-trained chef Craig has honed his craft working with David Everitt-Matthias at Le Champignon Sauvage in Cheltenham, and with Eric Chavot at The Capital Hotel in Knightsbridge which has two Michelin stars. Having brought his considerable talent to Ulverston, Craig is the first and only chef in the area to have been awarded two AA rosettes.

The opulent bar in Virginia House's atmospheric gin parlour nods to old-world drinking dens and speakeasies; this is the place where craft botanicals, artisan mixology and friends mingle. There's an ever-changing menu for even the most discerning of gin enthusiasts, and the knowledgeable staff are devoted to creating the perfect cocktail with the bar's signature ingredient. And for a peaceful end to the day, head to one of the bright boudoirs to stay and make the most of the breakfast the following morning!

Craig and Louise invite guests to step into their world, which they are passionate about making the best it can be, so whether you're a fine dining connoisseur or a novice epicurean, you won't want to miss out on a visit.

Virginia House

AA

The Rosette Award for
Culinary Excellence
2017 - 2018

Virginia House
SMOKED DUCK BREAST WITH DAMSONS AND PISTACHIO DUKKHA

Chef Craig Sherrington, who created this recipe, draws inspiration from the world around him – handpicking and foraging for the very best produce and ingredients – which means that from the earthy to the delicate; the exotic to the native; field to fork, his dishes are in tune with nature.

Preparation time: 15 minutes, plus defrosting | Cooking time: approx. 45 minutes| Serves: 4

Ingredients

200g frozen damsons

2 duck breasts

Smoking chips

50g sugar

For the dukkha:

5g pistachios

5g flaked almonds

10g pecans

2g poppy seeds

1g cumin seeds

1g coriander seeds

5ml rapeseed oil

5ml honey

To serve:

A few micro leaves, to garnish

Salt and pepper

Method

First, take the damsons out of the freezer and leave to defrost. Preheat oven to 210°c. Remove excess fat from the duck breast and score the skin. Place the smoking chips in a roasting tray and cover with a cooling wire rack. Season the duck breasts with salt and pepper, then place skin-side down on the rack and cover the whole tray with tinfoil. Place the baking tray over a medium heat and allow the duck to smoke for 5 minutes, then remove from the heat.

Next, place an ovenproof sauté pan on the heat. Place the duck breast skin-side down in the hot pan and sear for 30 seconds, then turn and cook for a further 30 seconds. Turn again so it's skin-side down and put the pan in the oven for 7 minutes at 210°c, then remove and rest for 10 minutes.

Remove the damson stones by squeezing the defrosted damsons, then place the fruit in a heavy-bottomed pan with the sugar and cook on a medium heat until a syrupy consistency is achieved. Remove from the heat and blend in a jug blender, then pass through a fine sieve to achieve a smooth consistency, and allow to cool.

To make the dukkha

Mix the pistachios, almonds, pecans, poppy seeds, cumin, coriander, rapeseed oil and honey together. Lightly roast for a couple of minutes and allow to cool.

To serve

To present the dish, brush a 'swish' of damson purée onto the plate, cut the duck breast into chunks and place on top of purée, sprinkle with dukkha and garnish with a few micro leaves.

Flour POWER

The Watermill is one of the few working mills in Britain that still uses water power, and probably the only one that's pink! With tours, a vegetarian tea room, and a shop selling the mill produce as well as organic produce and giftware in the picturesque surroundings of Little Salkeld in the Eden Valley – The Watermill has something for everyone.

Current owners Phil and Cheryl have run The Watermill with Cheryl's son Elliot since 2014, after spending six months learning the ropes from previous owners. Along with the know-how to work in the mill and create longstanding favourite recipes from the flour produced, the couple also inherited the signature pink colour of the mill buildings, which were painted on their restoration in the 1970s. Today, the mill, the shop, and tea room enjoy regular local custom with the help of the staff that Cheryl trains herself in the art of traditional bread-making and other valuable skills.

The mill itself specialises in British flour, which is stone-ground to retain the nutrition and flavour that can be damaged by the heat of modern milling methods. They only use grains that are biodynamic – which is a stricter version of organic certification – and all from wheat, barley, rye and spelt sourced from just three British farms. The lower gluten content of the flours, because they're from British-grown grain rather than the foreign varieties used in commercial breads, makes them more suitable for everyone, and great tasting too of course!

The Watermill's flour (as well as oats, oatmeal and muesli) is sold in the onsite shop and also made into cakes, scones, bread and more for the vegetarian food served in the welcoming café. Other outlets from North Cumbria down to Manchester, including farm shops and health food shops, also sell The Watermill's products so you don't have to be nearby to sample a taste of the tradition and time-honoured knowledge that goes into the milling of these natural ingredients.

Whether you're walking or cycling the Coast to Coast route, visiting the nearby 4000 year old stone circle, or just fancy a hot drink and a freshly baked treat, The Watermill is a great place to stop off or enjoy a day out. For those interested in the techniques used by this traditional working mill there are tours, and you can even learn how to perfect your own loaves with bread-making classes using The Watermill's products at Keswick Cookery School.

The Watermill
TRADITIONAL BREAD

Our wholemeal and unbleached white flours are stoneground at our mill from organic and biodynamically grown English wheat. For our white flour, we separate the coarser outer parts of the grain leaving only the white centre; it's creamy-white in colour as we do not add a bleaching agent. Being from British grain, the flour is low in gluten and produces a more traditional loaf.

Preparation time: 25 minutes, plus 45 minutes proving time | Cooking time: 25-40 minutes |
Makes 2 x 1lb loaves or 1 x 2lb loaf

Ingredients

For white bread:

500g flour

10g dried yeast

7g salt

350ml water

For wholemeal bread:

550g flour

11g dried yeast

11g salt

440ml water

Method

Mix the flour, yeast and salt in a mixing bowl. Add the water and mix together into a well-combined, slightly sticky dough. If making by hand, place the dough on a lightly floured board or work surface. Knead the dough well for 10-15 minutes until the dough can be stretched quite far but holds together. Flours with lower gluten content need more kneading to develop the gluten and help the dough rise. If using a stand mixer with a dough hook attachment, mix for 10 minutes on a medium to high setting, ensuring that the dough is picked up and kneaded for at least half of the time.

Grease the bread tin well, making sure anywhere the bread will touch is covered, otherwise the loaf will stick to the sides or base when cooked. If making 2 x 1lb loaves, weigh the dough and split evenly into two. Shape the dough by flattening into a rectangle roughly the same width as the tin. Then roll up the dough tightly so as to not leave any pockets of air. If there are any cracks on the top, flatten the dough again and repeat the rolling process until the top is smooth (if you have to do this more than three times the dough may need more kneading). With the join on the bottom, tuck under the sides of the dough.

Place the dough in the tin and leave to rise in a warm place (near a preheated oven works well, but no hotter than 40°c) for approximately 45 minutes. Depending on the room temperature, this may take over an hour but never leave dough for more than two hours. The dough is proved when it has risen to the top of the tin at the sides and above the tin in the middle, and springs back when pressed gently. Meanwhile, preheat the oven to 220°c.

Bake at the top of the preheated oven for 25 minutes (for 1lb loaves) or 40 minutes (for 2lb loaves). Avoid opening the door until the loaves are cooked. Tip out of the tin and tap the bottom to check; it should sound hollow when done. If you're not sure, place back in the oven for a few more minutes.

To serve

Leave the bread to cool on a wire rack. Slice once cooled, butter, and tuck in!

Note: Using Bread Machines

In bread machines, lower gluten flours can sometimes overprove (the dough collapses). We recommend using the basic setting on your machine and substituting 150g of the wholemeal flour in this recipe with white flour. Alternatively, use the dough setting then bake in a conventional oven.

The Watermill
FRUIT SCONES

Our scones are made using our 85% self-raising flour. Once the grain has been stoneground in our mill, we sieve off most of the bran (the outer layers of the grain) to produce a lighter wholemeal flour. The reduced bran content makes for better baking but still leaves plenty of nutrition, colour and most importantly, flavour!

Preparation time: 10 minutes | Cooking time: 13-14 minutes | Makes about 6 scones

Ingredients

454g Watermill self-raising flour

28g cane sugar

113g margarine or sunflower spread

56g sultanas, soaked in warm orange juice (or similar amount of your choice of dried fruit)

2 eggs

2 tbsp plain yogurt

118ml whole milk

Method

Mix the flour and sugar in a mixing bowl then rub the margarine into the flour and sugar with your fingertips. Then add the sultanas, or alternative dried fruit.

In a separate bowl, beat the eggs and mix in the milk and yogurt. Add enough of the wet ingredients to the flour, sugar and butter to make a soft dough; there should be a little bit left which you can use later in the recipe.

On a floured surface, pat the dough with your hand to flatten to a height slightly lower than the scone cutter. Cut out rounds and place on a lightly floured baking tray.

Brush the tops with the remaining egg, milk and yogurt mixture.

Bake the scones at 180°c for 13-14 minutes.

To serve

Slice in half and add butter, jam and/or cream to your liking!

The DIRECTORY

These great businesses have supported the making of this book; please support and enjoy them.

The Apple Pie Café and Bakery
Rydal Road
Ambleside
Cumbria
LA22 9AN
Telephone: 015394 33679
Website: www.applepieambleside.co.uk
Bakery with take-out shop, spacious café serving delicious homemade meals and boutique B&B accommodation in a listed building overlooking the Bridge House in Ambleside.

Appleby Creamery Ltd.
Eden Valley Business Park
Appleby
Cumbria
CA16 6PL
Telephone: TBC (moving premises in March 2018)
Website: www.applebycreamery.co.uk
Championing the tradition of Cumbrian artisan cheese; experienced producers creating a range of handmade products.

Blacksmiths Arms
Broughton Mills
Broughton in Furness
Cumbria
LA20 6AX
Telephone: 01229 716824
Website:
www.theblacksmithsarms.com
Traditional Lakeland pub with a strong emphasis on contemporary food.

The Boathouse Bar & Restaurant
Windermere Marina
Bowness-on-Windermere
Cumbria
LA23 3JQ
Telephone: 015394 22785
Website: www.theboathouse-windermere.co.uk
Fresh food and fine wine in a contemporary, relaxed and informal setting overlooking the boats on Lake Windermere.

Cartmel Cheeses
1 Unsworth's Yard
Cartmel
Grange-over-Sands
LA11 6PN
Telephone: 015395 34307
Website: www.cartmelcheeses.co.uk
Purveyor of fine cheeses, fresh breads, cakes, chutneys and biscuits.

Carvetii Coffee Roasters
The Roastery
Threlkeld Business Park
Threlkeld
Cumbria
CA12 4SU
Telephone: 01768 776979
Website: www.carvetiicoffee.co.uk
Carvetii Coffee is an award-winning speciality coffee roaster, based in Threlkeld in the Lake District and established by expert coffee enthusiasts, Gareth and Angharad. Monthly coffee subscriptions are available online.

Dodds Restaurant
Rydal Road
Ambleside
Cumbria
LA22 9AN
Telephone: 015394 32134
Website: www.doddsrestaurant.co.uk
Friendly Ambleside restaurant open for lunch and evening meals from a menu of Italian-inspired dishes.

Dodgson Wood
Nibthwaite Grange Farm
Near Ulverston
LA12 8DB
Telephone: 01229 885663
Website: www.dodgsonwood.co.uk
Working farm specialising in conservation grazing, and selling fresh and frozen meat from rare breed sheep and cows raised on the farm in the Lake District.

First Floor Café
Lakeland
Alexandra Buildings
Windermere
Cumbria
LA23 1BQ
Telephone: 015394 88100
or 015394 47116
Website: www.firstfloorcafe.co.uk
Situated within Lakeland's flagship store in Windermere, First Floor Café is an ideal spot for locals, shoppers and visitors to take in stunning views and enjoy freshly made food throughout the day.

Forest Side
Keswick Road
Grasmere
Cumbria
LA22 9RN
Telephone: 015394 35250
Website: www.theforestside.com
A beautiful retreat surrounded by stunning Lake District landscapes, with luxurious rooms and Michelin-starred dining that uses the natural larder of the Cumbrian landscape.

Fyne Fish
11 Station Street
Cockermouth
Cumbria CA13 9QW
Telephone: 01900 827814
Website: www.fynefish.net
Award-winning independent fishmongers featuring a large 'ready to eat' seafood deli selection, and specialising in bespoke seafood platters and freshly made sushi.

Hawkshead Brewery
Mill Yard
Staveley
Cumbria
LA8 9LR
Telephone: 01539 822644
Websites:
www.hawksheadbrewery.co.uk
Brewers of an eclectic range of distinctive, flavourful beers, based in the heart of the Lake District.

Hawkshead Relish Company
The Square
Hawkshead
Cumbria
LA22 0NZ
Telephone: 015394 36614
Website: www.hawksheadrelish.com
Artisan producers of quality, multi-award winning relishes, pickles and preserves.

Higginsons of Grange
Keswick House
Main Street
Grange-over-Sands
Cumbria
LA11 6AB
Telephone: 01539 534367
Website:
www.higginsonsofgrange.co.uk
Award-winning butchers and pie makers, showcasing the finest Cumbrian produce including speciality fresh meats, award-winning sausages, home-cured bacon and delicious cooked foods to take home, not to mention their famous hand-made pies.

L'al Churrasco
23-25 Market Street
Ulverston
Cumbria
LA12 7LR
Telephone: 01229 343160
Website: www.lalchurrasco.co.uk
Restaurant serving fresh Spanish, Portuguese and Southern Mediterranean tapas; bringing something out of the ordinary to Ulverston and the South Furness area.

Mrs Miller's Culgaith
Hazel Dene Garden Centre
Culgaith
Penrith
CA10 1QF
Telephone: 017688 82520
Website: www.mrsmillersculgaith.co.uk
North-West Local Restaurant of the Year in the Waitrose Good Food Guide and a fantastic spot to enjoy breakfast, lunch, or an evening meal on Fridays and Saturdays from the daily changing menu based on the freshest and best local produce.

The Old Stamp House
Church Street
Ambleside
Cumbria
LA22 0BU
Telephone: 01539 432775
Website: www.oldstamphouse.com
Award-winning restaurant inspired by the food culture and heritage of Cumbria.

Poppi Red
Main Street
Hawkshead
Cumbria
LA22 0NT
Telephone: 015394 36434
Website: www.poppi-red.co.uk
Distinctive, warm and welcoming gift shop and café with cakes, pastries and lunch menu in the village of Hawkshead.

The Porterage Co. Cumbria Ltd.
Unit 4b Crakeside Business Park
Greenodd
Ulverston
Cumbria
LA12 7RT
Telephone: 01229 861088

The Porterage Co. Windermere
Belmont House
Lakes Road
Bowness-on-Windermere
LA23 3BJ
Telephone: 015394 45442
Website: www.theporterage.co.uk
Independent wine merchant supplying hotels, restaurants and the general public with a friendly and reliable shopping experience for wines, spirits, craft ales and other fantastic local accompaniments.

Porto Restaurant
3 Ash Street
Bowness-on-Windermere
LA23 3EB
Telephone: 015394 48242
Website: www.porto-restaurant.co.uk
Award-winning modern British food and excellent service, to be enjoyed in elegant dining rooms or on the heated roof terrace.

Rothay Manor Hotel & Fine Dining
Rothay Road
Ambleside
Cumbria
LA22 0EH
Telephone: 015394 33605
Website: www.rothaymanor.co.uk
Warm and friendly country house hotel with fine dining restaurant.

Shed 1 Distillery
Telephone: 07397 180486
Website: www.shed1distillery.com
Small batch gin-maker working from an actual garden shed in Ulverston, Cumbria. Husband and wife team Andy and Zoe create smooth, bold flavoured gins with a growing list of stockists.

Slate Bar & Café
5 Wainwrights Yard
Kendal
Cumbria
LA9 4DP
Telephone: 01539 232105
Website: www.slatebar.co.uk
Warm and welcoming café bar in Kendal serving coffee, cocktails and light lunch options including charcuterie, cheese and artisan bread throughout the day and evening.

The Square Orange
20 St John's Street
Keswick
Cumbria
CA12 5AS
Telephone: 017687 73888
Website: www.thesquareorange.co.uk
Keswick café bar with a continental feel and a warm, lively welcome. Serving local and European beers on tap as well as food all day, including stonebaked pizza, tapas, antipasti, mezze and more.

Stockghyll Fine Foods
Central Buildings
Rydal Road
Ambleside
Lake District
LA22
Telephone: 015394 31865
Website: www.stockghyllfinefood.co.uk
Family-run delicatessen celebrating quality produce, freshly made food and specialist ingredients from Cumbria and beyond.

Virginia House
24 Queen Street
Ulverston
LA12 7AF
Telephone: 01229 584844
Website:
www.virginiahouseulverston.co.uk
Intimate fine dining restaurant with seasonal, multi-course tasting menus, an atmospheric gin parlour and rooms.

The Watermill
Little Salkeld
Penrith
Cumbria
CA10 1NN
Telephone: 01768 881 523
Website: www.organicmill.co.uk
An 18th century watermill milling organic and biodynamic stoneground British flours with a vegetarian tearoom and shop selling mill produce, organic groceries and giftware, easily found ten minutes from junction 40 of the M6 in the picturesque Eden Valley.

INDEX

Other titles in the 'Get Stuck In' series

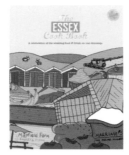

The Essex Cook Book features Thomas Leatherbarrow, The Anchor Riverside, Great Garnetts, Deersbrook Farm, Mayfield Bakery and lots more.
978-1-910863-25-1

The South London Cook Book features Jose Pizarro, Adam Byatt, The Alma, Piccalilli Caff, Canopy Beer, Inkspot Brewery and lots more.
978-1-910863-27-5

The Bristol Cook Book features Dean Edwards, Lido, Clifton Sausage, The Ox, and wines from Corks of Cotham plus lots more.
978-1-910863-14-5

The Oxfordshire Cook Book features Mike North of The Nut Tree Inn, Sudbury House, Jacobs Inn, The Muddy Duck and lots more.
978-1-910863-08-4

The Brighton & Sussex Cook Book features Steven Edwards, The Bluebird Tea Co, Isaac At, Real Patisserie, Sussex Produce Co, and lots more.
978-1-910863-22-0

The Liverpool Cook Book features Burnt Truffle, The Art School, Fraîche, Villaggio Cucina and many more.
978-1-910863-15-2

The Sheffield Cook Book - Second Helpings features Jameson's Tea Rooms, Craft & Dough, The Wortley Arms, The Holt, Grind Café and lots more.
978-1-910863-16-9

The Leeds Cook Book features The Boxtree, Crafthouse, Stockdales of Yorkshire and lots more.
978-1-910863-18-3

The Cotswolds Cook Book features David Everitt-Matthias of Champignon Sauvage, Prithvi, Chef's Dozen and lots more.
978-0-9928981-9-9

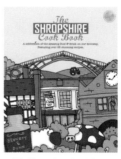

The Shropshire Cook Book features Chris Burt of The Peach Tree, Old Downton Lodge, Shrewsbury Market, CSons and lots more.
978-1-910863-32-9

The Norfolk Cook Book features Richard Bainbridge, Morston Hall, The Duck Inn and lots more.
978-1-910863-01-5

The Lincolnshire Cook Book features Colin McGurran of Winteringham Fields, TV chef Rachel Green, San Pietro and lots more.
978-1-910863-05-3

The Devon Cook Book sponsored by Food & Drink Devon features Simon Hulstone of The Elephant, Noel Corston, Riverford Field Kitchen & much more.
978-1-910863-24-4

The Cheshire Cook Book features Simon Radley of The Chester Grosvenor, The Chef's Table, Great North Pie Co., Harthill Cookery School and lots more.
978-1-910863-07-7

The Leicestershire & Rutland Cook Book features Tim Hart of Hambleton Hall, John's House, Farndon Fields, Leicester Market, Walter Smith and lots more.
978-0-9928981-8-2

All books in this series are available from Waterstones, Amazon and independent bookshops.

FIND OUT MORE ABOUT US AT WWW.MEZEPUBLISHING.CO.UK